EYEWITNESS
ANCIENT EGYPT

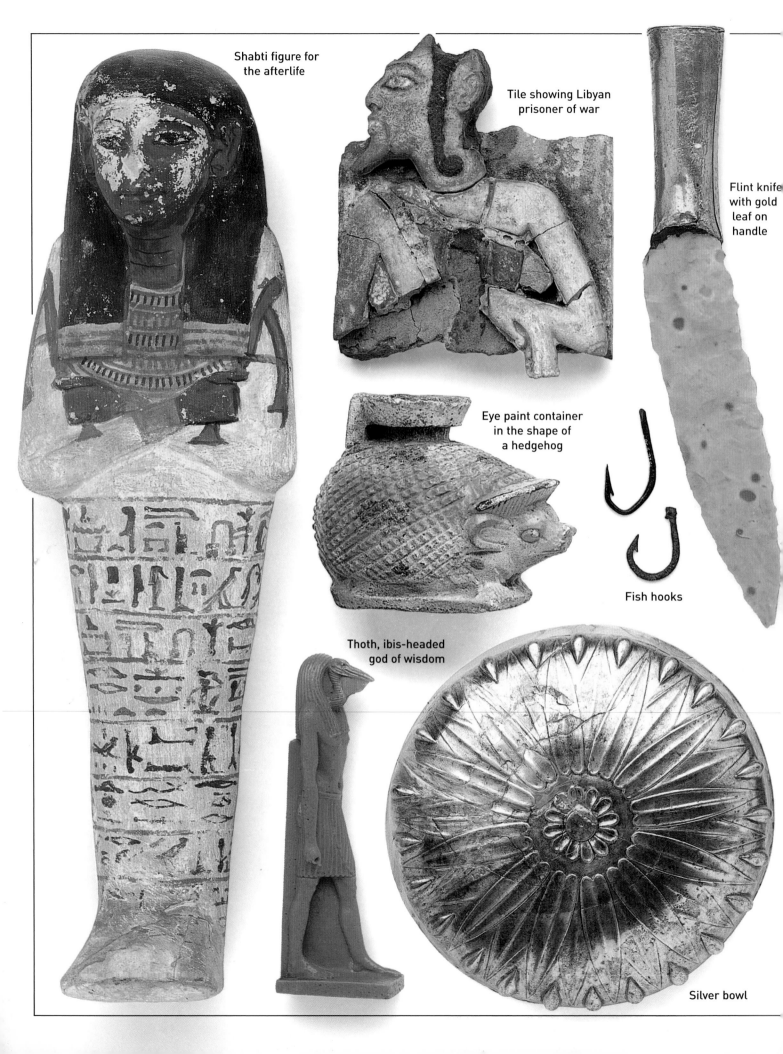

Shabti figure for the afterlife

Tile showing Libyan prisoner of war

Flint knife with gold leaf on handle

Eye paint container in the shape of a hedgehog

Fish hooks

Thoth, ibis-headed god of wisdom

Silver bowl

Fish amulet
hair pendants

EYEWITNESS
ANCIENT
EGYPT

Written by
GEORGE HART

Gold plaque
showing
pharaoh and
Sun-god Aten

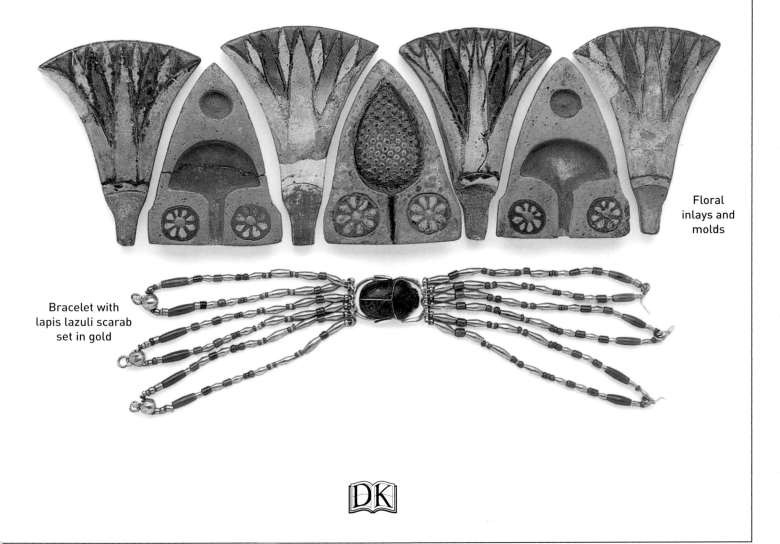

Floral
inlays and
molds

Bracelet with
lapis lazuli scarab
set in gold

DK

Paddle doll

Earrings

Penguin Random House

Project editor Phil Wilkinson
Designer Thomas Keenes
Senior editor Sophie Mitchell
Senior art editor Julia Harris
Editorial director Sue Unstead
Art director Anne-Marie Bulat
Special photography Peter Hayman of The Department
of Egyptian Antiquities, British Museum

RELAUNCH EDITION (DK UK)
Editor Ashwin Khurana
US editor Margaret Parrish
Senior designers Rachael Grady, Spencer Holbrook
Managing editor Gareth Jones
Managing art editor Philip Letsu
Publisher Andrew Macintyre
Producer, preproduction Adam Stoneham
Senior producer Charlotte Cade
Jacket editor Maud Whatley
Jacket designer Laura Brim
Jacket design development manager Sophia MTT
Publishing director Jonathan Metcalf
Associate publishing director Liz Wheeler
Art director Phil Ormerod

RELAUNCH EDITION (DK INDIA)
Editor Surbhi Nayyar Kapoor
Art editors Deep Shikha Walia, Shreya Sadhan
Senior DTP designer Harish Aggarwal
DTP designers Anita Yadav, Pawan Kumar
Managing editor Alka Thakur Hazarika
Managing art editor Romi Chakraborty
CTS manager Balwant Singh
Jacket editorial manager Saloni Talwar
Jacker designers Govind Mittal, Suhita Dharamjit,
Vikas Chauhan

First American Edition, 1990
This American Edition, 2014
Published in the United States by DK Publishing
4th floor, 345 Hudson Street
New York, New York 10014

17 18 10 9 8 7 6
012-196432—07/14

A catalog record for this book is available
from the Library of Congress.

ISBN 978-1-4654-2048-0 (Paperback)
ISBN 978-1-4654-2090-9 (ALB)

DK books are available at special discounts when purchased in
bulk for sales promotions, premiums, fund-raising, or educational
use. For details, contact: DK Publishing Special Markets,
345 Hudson Street, New York, New York 10014
or SpecialSale@dk.com.

Color reproduction by Alta Image Ltd., UK
Printed in China

Discover more at

www.dk.com

Wooden cosmetic spoon

Glass tube and applicator for eye paint

Glass ear studs

Pendant of lapis lazuli bull's head set in gold

Contents

Sketch on flake of limestone

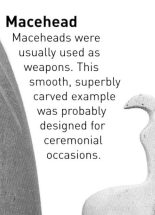

Macehead
Maceheads were usually used as weapons. This smooth, superbly carved example was probably designed for ceremonial occasions.

Early Egypt

In the early Stone Age, people in Egypt lived high up on the land above the Nile. By about 5000 BCE, they had become farmers, growing wheat and barley and raising cattle. They also built villages of mud huts in parts of the flood plain. The farmers prospered and started to form kingdoms. Recent excavation shows that by 3500 BCE, people were already living in cities and had started to invent systems of writing. Objects found in brick-lined graves, such as beautifully carved ivories, slate palettes, and clay pots reveal fascinating details of life in Egypt before the pharaohs came to power in c. 3100 BCE.

Comb and companion
The African elephant and hippo provided plenty of ivory for early craftworkers. The figure with the striking eyes was placed in a tomb to provide the owner with a companion in the afterlife.

Ancient body
Before mummification, bodies were buried in a "sleeping" position in a sandy pit. The sand dried and preserved the body, so that a person's spirit would be able to recognize it. This man died about 5,000 years ago. His features and ginger hair have been fairly well preserved.

Food containers useful in the afterlife

Skin well preserved because body was dried out by sand

Ginger hair

Necklaces

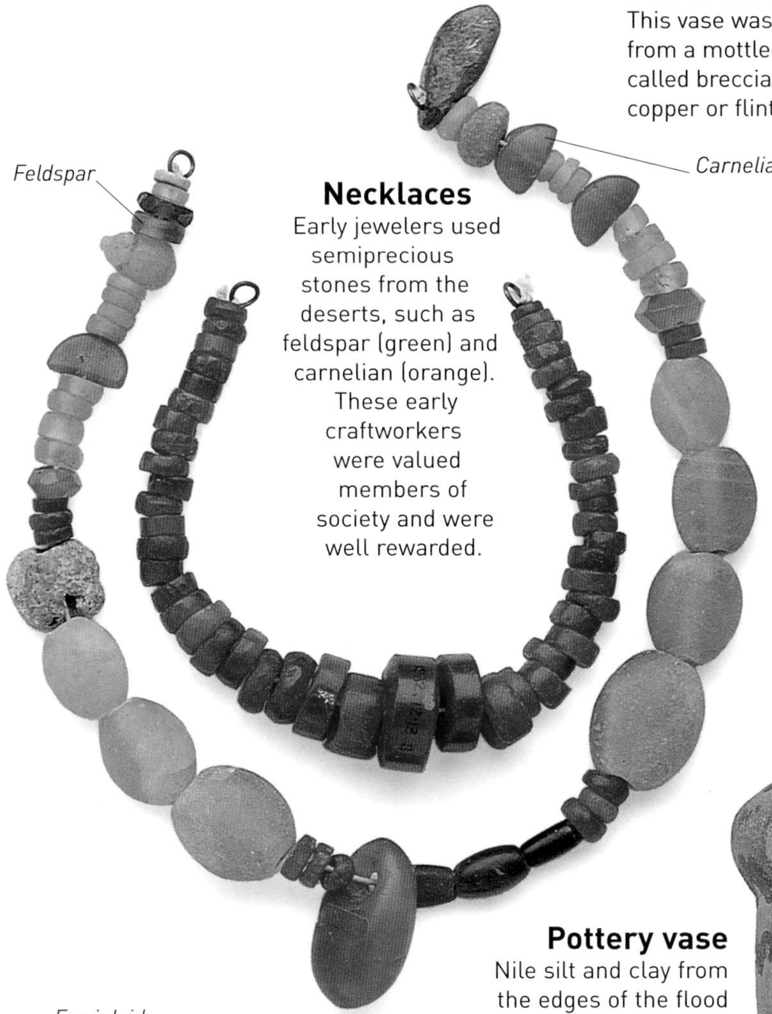

Stone vase

This vase was carved from a mottled stone called breccia, using copper or flint tools.

Carnelian

Feldspar

Necklaces

Early jewelers used semiprecious stones from the deserts, such as feldspar (green) and carnelian (orange). These early craftworkers were valued members of society and were well rewarded.

Smooth shape made by simple tools

Pottery vase

Nile silt and clay from the edges of the flood plain provided materials for the early potters. This pot's tapering base was designed to fit in a stand or in a hollow in the ground.

Eye inlaid with ivory

Spiral design

Cosmetic palette

Some of the earliest surviving Egyptian objects are slate palettes. They could be rectangular, or carved in animal shapes, such as hippos, turtles, falcons, or this obese ram. The surface was used for grinding minerals for eye paint (see p. 58).

Life on the Nile

Desert covers more than 90 percent of Egypt and the climate is hot and dry. Egyptian civilization was only able to flourish thanks to the Nile River, which flooded once a year, spreading rich, dark silt across the fields. Most Egyptians lived on the banks of the Nile in a fertile area called "Kemet" or the "Black Land." The barren desert beyond this strip of farmland was called the "Red Land." The farming year began with the Nile's annual flood. When the waters finally retreated, the farmers got to work sowing barley, flax, and emmer wheat. The result was usually a good summer harvest.

Famine
This statue shows a man begging for food. The extreme climate meant that the crops sometimes failed, leading to famine.

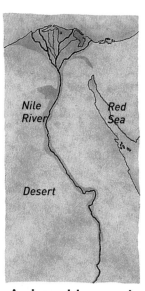

A riverside people
The Egyptians lived on a fertile strip on each side of the Nile. The flood plain is shown in green.

Scribe with his palette

Herdsman driving cattle with a stick

Sickle

Farmers cut the crops using simple tools, such as this wooden sickle with flint teeth. The stalks left behind would be gathered to make mats and baskets.

Flint cutting edge

Winnowing

The grain and chaff were thrown into the air so that the lighter husks were blown away, leaving the grain to fall to the floor. This process is called winnowing.

Winnowing fan

Two wooden fans like this one were used to separate the grain from the chaff (husk).

Shaduf

The farmers dug canals to transport water to the fields. To raise the water to fill the canals, the Egyptians used a device called a shaduf (a trellis supporting a pole with a counterweight). The bucket was lowered into the river then pulled up with the help of the weight.

Cattle counting

In ancient Egypt, wealth was measured by the number of cattle a person owned. This tomb model shows Meketre, the mayor of Thebes in c. 2000 BCE. The town's officials are counting his cattle for tax records.

Meketre, owner of the cattle

Meketre's son

Famous pharaohs

The oval enclosing the hieroglyphs that spell out a pharaoh's name is called a cartouche.

From c. 3100 BCE, Egypt was ruled by powerful kings known as pharaohs. The title pharaoh comes from the words *per-aa* meaning "great house," which refers to the king's palace. The pharaoh was believed to be a living god and his queen was a goddess, although she was usually given the title of "Great Royal Wife." Only rarely did women rule Egypt in their own right. On the king's death the throne passed to his son, who would be specially trained in sports and warfare to prepare him for the role. Princes sometimes had to wait a long time to take power. One pharaoh, Pepy II, came to the throne at the age of six. He was still king 94 years later.

Armless queen
This statue shows a queen of Egypt from c. 700 BCE. The statue's arms have been lost.

Osiris, god of the underworld

Akhenaten

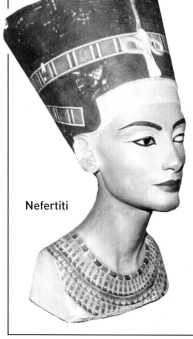

Hatshepsut
Queen Hatshepsut (above) ruled Egypt for about 20 years. She was supposed to be ruling on behalf of her young stepson, but declared herself pharaoh in 1473 BCE.

Nefertiti

Akhenaten and Nefertiti
In Akhenaten's reign, the traditional Egyptian gods were banished—only the Sun-god Aten was worshiped. Akhenaten, who ruled with his wife Nefertiti, founded a new capital city and closed the temples of the other gods. After their death, their names became hated and their temples were destroyed. Eventually the old gods were restored by Tutankhamun.

Sphinxes

In ancient Egypt, the sphinx was a mythological creature with a lion's body and the head of a ruler. Lions were associated with the Sun-god and their strength represented the pharaoh's power. Sometimes sphinxes combined other elements, such as the head and wings of a hawk, which symbolized the god Horus. Monumental statues of sphinxes were often placed in front of tombs to guard the pharaoh in the afterlife.

Sphinx at Giza
This sphinx was carved around 4,500 years ago for the pharaoh Khafre.

In control
This ivory statuette shows a sphinx representing the pharaoh's power.

Ceremonial beard

Cobra goddess

Head cloth

Ramesses the Great
In the 13th century BCE, Ramesses II reigned for 67 years. He built a vast number of monuments, including a temple at Thebes, now called the Ramesseum. This statue shows him wearing a royal headcloth called the "nemes," under a crown of cobras.

Jar of sacred liquid

Tutankhamun
This ruler came to the throne at the age of nine. He was determined to bring back the old gods who had been banished by Akhenaten (see left). This famous golden mask was found in his tomb (see p. 23).

(see p. 23)

Tuthmosis IV
This king was famous for clearing the sand that had buried the Great Sphinx at Giza. He is shown holding jars of sacred liquid and wearing a headcloth featuring the cobra goddess Wadjet. It was believed that Wadjet protected the pharaoh by spitting fire at his enemies.

Royal court

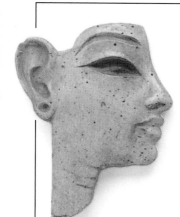

Royal head
This glass portrait probably decorated an item of furniture or a window.

At great state occasions, such as jubilee celebrations or the presentation of gifts to favored courtiers, the king and court gathered together, and top officials, diplomats, and high priests would attend. Some courtiers were relatives of the king. Others were high-ranking army officers or head scribes. Pharaohs were all powerful and commanded great respect. When people approached the king, they would often kiss the ground beneath his feet.

Fishes
Egyptian children often wore fish-shaped amulets in their hair.

Amulet case
Protective amulets could be put in a case and hung from a necklace.

Oyster pendant
Early Egyptian jewelry was often made of shells. Later, jewelers copied these shapes in gold.

Lion's-paw legs

Royal throne
Queen Hetepheres was the mother of King Khufu (see p. 20). Her court throne was made of wood overlaid with gold leaf. Insects ate the wood away, but archeologists were able to reconstruct the furniture.

Throwstick
Courtiers used wooden throwsticks to catch birds. This one, made of brittle faience (see p. 47), was a ceremonial throwstick. It bears the name of the pharaoh Akhenaten.

Royal vases
The pharaohs used the best quality utensils, which were buried in their tombs for use in the next world. These two carved stone vases have gold lids adorned with imitation twine, also in gold. They were made for King Khasekhemwy.

Eye of Horus (see p. 24), meant to indicate the object's good condition

Name of King Akhenaten

God of "millions of years" holding branches in his hands

Dog-headed scepter

Bouquet

Noblewoman

Wives of great officials held high status at court. They often formed themselves into a group called a guild, protected by the goddess Hathor. This woman wears a heavy wig adorned with a circle of flowers.

Sign of life

Only gods, kings, and queens were allowed to carry the ankh, the Egyptian symbol of life. It indicates that the holder has the power to give life or take it away.

Pillar of the god Osiris

Pharaoh

This gold figurine shows the royal crown decorated with the cobra goddess, and the crook and flail, which represent kingship.

Lotus tile

This tile comes from a piece of furniture in King Akhenaten's palace. Surviving fragments like this give us an idea of the splendors of the royal courts.

Finely pleated dress

Lotus design

Mummies

A scarab was placed over a king's heart to protect him in the underworld.

The Egyptians believed in an afterlife where they would be reborn in their original bodies. For this to happen, the body had to be preserved by mummifying it. The inner organs were removed, dried, and stored in vessels called canopic jars. The heart was left behind so that it could be weighed in the afterlife (see p. 19). Then the body was dried with natron salt and wrapped in linen bandages.

Anubis
The god Anubis was responsible for embalming. Here, he puts the final touches on a mummified body.

Instrument for touching the mouth

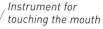

Vase

Wax plate
Plates like this one, decorated with the eye of Horus (see p. 24), were used to cover cuts made in the flesh of the corpse.

"Opening the Mouth" utensils
One of the most important of all funerary rites, this ceremony was thought to bring a mummy to life, allowing it to eat, drink, and move. This model kit contains some of the instruments for the ceremony, including vases and cups for the sacred liquids and a forked instrument for touching the mouth.

Ritual and spell
Priests scatter purified water and touch the mouth of the upright mummy case with the ritual instruments. The eldest son burns incense and a spell is recited.

Canopic jars
These special containers were meant to protect the organs from spells. The intestines, stomach, liver, and lungs were each placed in a separate jar.

Mummy labels
Small, wooden tags were used to identify mummies. Anubis is shown in black on the left. Black was a symbol of life in Egypt because it was the color of the fertile Nile mud.

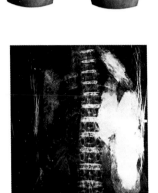

Inside a mummy
An X-ray reveals the stuffing that replaced the organs.

Natron
Natron salt was used to dry out the corpse. The crystals were packed around the body and within 40 days it would have dried out and no further decay would take place. It was then ready for bandaging.

Ancient linen wrapping

Unwrapped
This mummy shows how well the natron has preserved the body—even the toenails are intact.

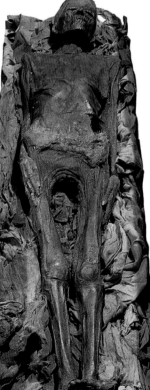

Everlasting bodies

The final stage in the embalming process was to put the body in its coffin. Wealthy people often had elaborate coffins, made up of several decorated layers. The Egyptians believed that two important spirits lived on after a person's death. The most important was the "Ka," which would bring the corpse back to life. Another spirit that lived on after death was a person's "Ba," which was represented by a hawk with a human head. The process of mummification was intended to make a body last forever and to provide the Ka with a home in the afterlife.

Hand and arm from an Egyptian mummy

Ramesses III
The body of Ramesses III, who ruled over Egypt in the 12th century BCE, shows his eyes packed with linen and his arms still positioned as if holding the crook and flail scepters (see p. 13).

(see p. 13)

Mummy case
Once it was wrapped in linen bandages, the body was free from decay. The interior of the coffin could be richly decorated with images of gods, while the outside would be adorned with colorful hieroglyphs of spells destined to help the dead person in the kingdom of Osiris, god of the underworld.

Idealized portrait of the deceased

Red straps usually indicate a member of the priesthood

Sun disk

Sky goddess Nut

Falcon

Linen protects body

Spells written in hieroglyphs

Mummified head

This is what a mummy looks like when the linen layers are peeled back. The technique of embalming used in ancient Egypt was remarkable, but it made the flesh look withered and discolored. The eyes were destroyed by the natron, so pads of linen were put in the eye sockets and the lids were closed over these. The nose could also be damaged as a result of pressure from the linen wrappings. The linen often stuck to the skin because of the oils applied to the body.

Eyes stuffed with linen pads

Linen wrappings still sticking to skin

Damage to the nose, perhaps caused by tight wrappings

Teeth with worn caps because of coarse Egyptian bread (see p. 48)

17

The afterlife

The ancient Egyptians believed that below the earth there was an underworld called Duat—a place full of dangers, such as fiery lakes and poisonous snakes. To protect against these perils, spells were written on coffins or on ornate papyrus scrolls. If you could recite the correct spells, you would be able to pass through Duat unharmed. The ultimate danger was to fail the test set in the Hall of the Two Truths, where your heart was weighed against your past deeds. If you passed the test, you could go through to a land that was just like Egypt itself.

Outspread arms show the god's power extended beyond its own body

Ram-headed god statue covered in black resin

Hired mourners
Women were sometimes hired to weep at funerals, since the number of mourners reflected the status of the deceased.

Ram-headed god
Sometimes statues of the underworld gods were taken into the tombs of the Valley of the Kings (see p. 22). They were meant to protect the king as he traveled through the underworld. These gods had heads of creatures such as tortoises, hippos, or rams.

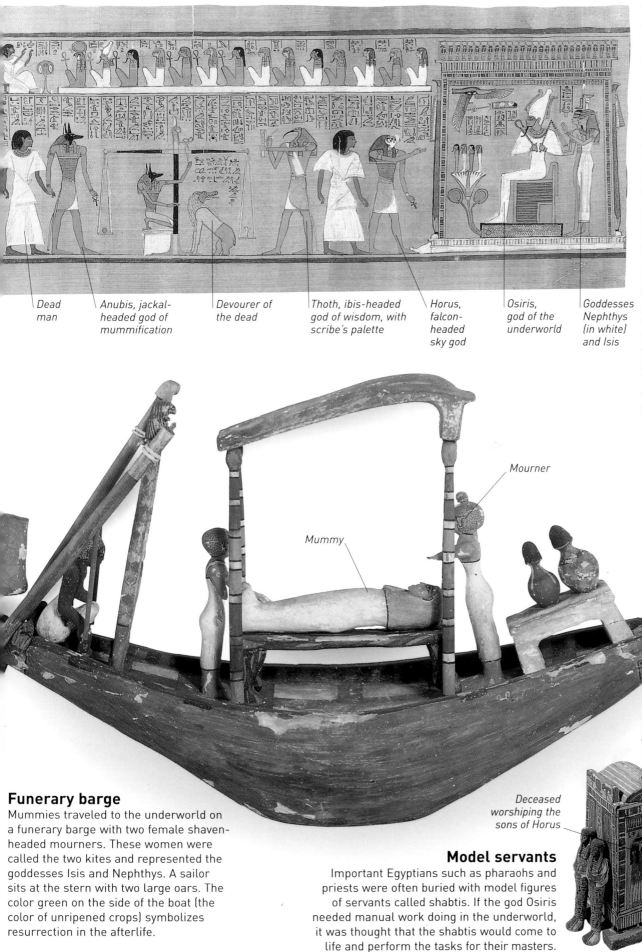

Weighing the heart

Here, the heart of the dead man is placed on the scales to be weighed against the feather of truth. If his heart weighs less than the feather, he can go to the kingdom of Osiris and be reborn. If his heart is heavier than the feather, it means that he is evil or untruthful. His heart will then be fed to the goddess Ammut, the "Devourer of the Dead" and he will not survive into the afterlife. Thoth, the god of wisdom, records the result.

Dead man

Anubis, jackal-headed god of mummification

Devourer of the dead

Thoth, ibis-headed god of wisdom, with scribe's palette

Horus, falcon-headed sky god

Osiris, god of the underworld

Goddesses Nephthys (in white) and Isis

Mourner

Mummy

Funerary barge

Mummies traveled to the underworld on a funerary barge with two female shaven-headed mourners. These women were called the two kites and represented the goddesses Isis and Nephthys. A sailor sits at the stern with two large oars. The color green on the side of the boat (the color of unripened crops) symbolizes resurrection in the afterlife.

Deceased worshiping the sons of Horus

Model servants

Important Egyptians such as pharaohs and priests were often buried with model figures of servants called shabtis. If the god Osiris needed manual work doing in the underworld, it was thought that the shabtis would come to life and perform the tasks for their masters.

The pyramids

The first pyramid was built as the tomb of King Djoser in c. 2650 BCE, by his architect Imhotep (see p. 34). Called the Step Pyramid, it rose in six stages and was designed as a gigantic stairway to the Sun-god in the sky. Pyramids with sloping sides were built during the reign of King Sneferu to represent the mound on which the Sun-god stood at the beginning of time. The largest pyramid is the Great Pyramid at Giza, built for King Khufu in c. 2589 BCE. The pyramids were built to protect the bodies and treasures of the pharaohs and had granite doors and false passages to deter thieves. But by c. 1000 BCE almost all of the pyramids had been robbed.

Grand Gallery
This gallery, 154 ft (47 m) long and 28 ft (8.5 m) high, rises toward the burial chamber. Its magnificent roof is built of stone. After the burial, great blocks of granite were lowered down the slope to seal off the chamber.

Climbers
In the 19th-century, many visitors climbed the Great Pyramid to admire the view below. Today, it is illegal to climb the pyramids in Egypt.

Small pyramids, the burial places of the three chief wives of Khufu

Mortuary temple, where offerings could be made

The Great Pyramid
Built for King Khufu around 4,500 years ago, the Great Pyramid was one of the Seven Wonders of the World. It took about 20 years to build and contains over 2.3 million limestone blocks ranging from 2.8 to 16.5 tons (2.5 to 15 metric tons) in weight. The builders may have used levers to get the stones into place, but had no pulleys or other machinery. Every year, field workers joined the workforce for three months during the Nile flood. The complex also contained a mortuary temple for offerings, and a causeway leading to the valley temple where the king's body was received after its last journey along the Nile.

Causeway connecting pyramid to temple in Nile valley

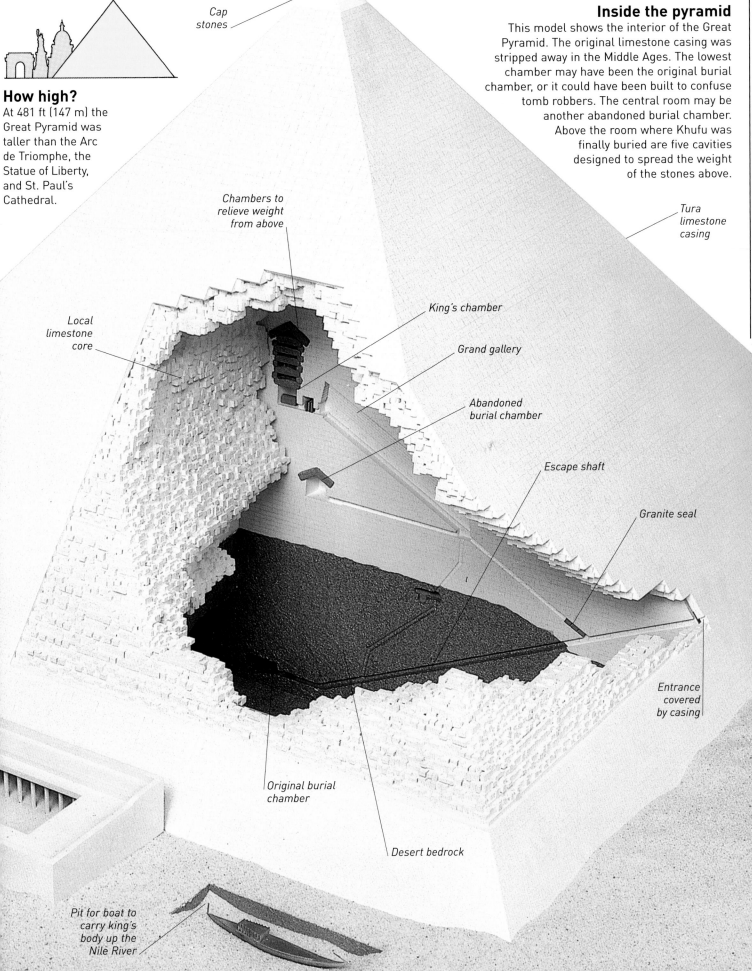

How high?
At 481 ft (147 m) the Great Pyramid was taller than the Arc de Triomphe, the Statue of Liberty, and St. Paul's Cathedral.

Cap stones

Inside the pyramid
This model shows the interior of the Great Pyramid. The original limestone casing was stripped away in the Middle Ages. The lowest chamber may have been the original burial chamber, or it could have been built to confuse tomb robbers. The central room may be another abandoned burial chamber. Above the room where Khufu was finally buried are five cavities designed to spread the weight of the stones above.

Tura limestone casing

Chambers to relieve weight from above

Local limestone core

King's chamber

Grand gallery

Abandoned burial chamber

Escape shaft

Granite seal

Entrance covered by casing

Original burial chamber

Desert bedrock

Pit for boat to carry king's body up the Nile River

The Valley of the Kings

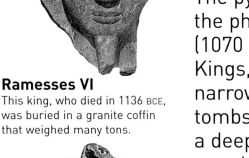

Ramesses VI
This king, who died in 1136 BCE, was buried in a granite coffin that weighed many tons.

The pyramid age came to an end in c. 2150 BCE. Nearly all the pharaohs from Tuthmosis I (1504 BCE) to Ramesses XI (1070 BCE) chose to be buried in tombs in the Valley of the Kings, which lay deep in the cliffs west of the Nile. The narrow entrance to the valley could be guarded, and some tombs were hidden high in the cliffs. Tombs usually had a deep corridor known as the Way of the Sun-God, which had a well near the inner end to catch rainwater and to deter tomb robbers. Beyond this was the Hall of Gold, where the king would be buried, surrounded by gilded furniture, jewelry, royal clothing, and other treasures.

Underworld deity
This hippo-headed god was found in the tomb of Tuthmosis III. It is covered in black resin because black was the color of life in ancient Egypt. It probably represented a guardian of the house of Osiris, god of the underworld.

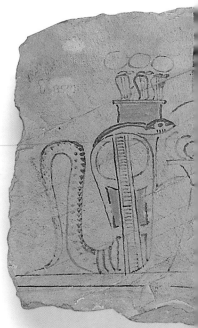

Sacred serpent
The Valley of the Kings was thought to be protected by the cobra goddess, Meretseger. Tomb workers believed that she had the power to blind or poison liars and criminals.

Valley view
This painting of the Valley of the Kings by 19th-century artist David Roberts shows a quiet, remote place. Today, it is much busier, with a modern road, parking lot, and souvenir stalls.

Foreman and his son

Foremen like Anherkhau, shown here with his son, were responsible for organizing the workflow in the tomb and making sure that the workers had the correct tools. This picture of Anherkhau comes from his own colorfully painted tomb.

Unknown king

The statue of this unknown king was found in the tomb of Tutankhamun. The monarch wears the "Red Crown" showing authority over Lower Egypt and holds the royal crook and flail.

Deir el Medina

These stone foundations belong to the village where the tomb workers lived. Founded in the 16th century BCE, it flourished for 500 years. Usually about 60 families lived in these houses at any one time.

Tutankhamun

The tomb of Tutankhamun was the only one in the valley to escape almost untouched by robbers. Discovered by Howard Carter in 1922, it was the last valley tomb to be found. It contained weapons, furniture, jewelry, and model boats, as well as the king's famous coffins and mask (see p. 11). Many of these items were made of solid gold or were richly decorated with gold leaf. The king was buried with his two stillborn daughters and a lock of his grandmother's hair.

All dressed up

The contents of Tutankhamun's tomb were transported to Cairo Museum. Here, archeologists Lord Carnarvon and Howard Carter are wrapping one of the guardian statues from the tomb.

Egyptian gods

The Egyptians worshiped hundreds of different deities (gods and goddesses). Each district had its own gods, many of which were represented by animals. The most powerful god was the Sun-god, who was worshiped in many different forms, including Khepri (the scarab beetle), Re-Harakhty (the Sun-hawk), and Amun-Re (king of the gods and protector of the pharaoh). During his reign, the pharaoh Akhenaten declared the Sun-god Aten as the god of the royal court and banned all other gods. They were restored by his son Tutankhamun (see p. 10).

Egyptian workshop

This 19th-century scene shows figures of the gods being made. The cat models for an image of Bastet (opposite).

Wadjet eye

Wadjet eye

Ibis

Scarab

Amulets

Charms called amulets provided protection against evil. The "wadjet" eye symbolized both the vengeful eye of the Sun-god and the eye of the god Horus. The scarab beetle symbolized the Sun-god Khepri, who pushed the Sun across the sky at dawn. The sacred ibis represented Thoth, the god of wisdom and healing.

Amun-re

Amun-Re (right) became king of the gods in New Kingdom times (1550–1086 BCE). He had a mysterious nature, which even the other gods were unaware of. The word "Amun" means "hidden."

Thoth

The Moon god Thoth (below) was responsible for medicine, mathematics, and writing. He was also the patron of scribes. His symbol was the ibis.

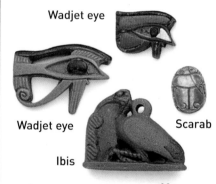

Winged scarab

Anubis

Jackals used to haunt cemeteries, so the jackal-headed god Anubis became closely linked with the dead. Anubis also supervised embalming (see p. 14).

Gods of wealth

Often called the "Nile gods," these figures were symbols of the fertility that came from the river's annual flood.

Horus

The sky god Horus was shown with the head of a hawk. The Egyptians believed that the pharaoh was the "living Horus" and was therefore a god himself. This relief shows Tuthmosis III in front of the god.

Bastet

The cat goddess Bastet represented the power of the Sun to ripen crops. Many bronze cat figures were dedicated to her.

Osiris

Osiris was the god of the underworld and the afterlife. His kingdom below the earth was thought to look something like Egypt.

Crook and flail sceptres, showing that Osiris is king of the underworld

Crown of reeds and ostrich feathers

Silver necklace with wadjet eye

Scarab

Khnum

The ram-headed god Khnum looked after the Nile's waterfalls. He ordered the god Hapy to cause the river's annual flood.

Healing the sick

The ancient Egyptians had great faith in magic and medicine. Egyptian doctors wrote manuals that show a detailed knowledge of anatomy. They also describe how to treat a variety of ailments such as fevers, tumors, and eye disorders. Doctors and magicians worked together, using medicines, plants, and spells to cure illness and ward off evil. Many people also wore special magical charms called amulets to protect them from danger.

Panel from the tomb of Hesire, the king's dentist in c. 2700 BCE

Amulets
Magical charms could be worn on necklaces and bracelets to ward off injury. They were also placed in mummy wrappings to give protection in the next life.

Pillar amulet

Knot amulet

Powerful plants

Plants played an important part in both magic and medicine. Many were very valuable—juniper berries were specially imported from Lebanon for their healing properties.

Lotus
The lotus was very important in Egypt, and images of its flower were often used to decorate temples.

Lotus blossom

Juniper berries
These were placed in the mummies of royalty or crocodiles. The juice was also used in rituals to purify the dead.

Hear our prayer
This stela contains a prayer to the god Ptah.

Henna
Henna was used to dye hair and skin, and ward off evil.

Garlic
This plant was thought to repel snakes and expel tapeworms.

Taweret
The goddess Taweret looked after women in childbirth. Shown as a ferocious, pregnant hippo, she was thought to keep evil away from a woman giving birth.

Serpent armed with knife

Jackal

Lion

Eye of Horus

Magical knife
The designs on these boomerang-shaped objects were thought to have great power. The knives were probably used to draw a magical protective barrier around vulnerable parts of a house.

Ready for sacrifice
This painting shows a calf adorned with a garland of flowers, ready to be sacrificed.

Papyrus calendar
The days shown in red on this calendar were seen as unlucky. The color red symbolized the dry deserts and was often used to represent bad fortune.

Tambourine

God of the family
Part-dwarf, part-lion, Bes was the god of newborn babies and of the family in general. A popular household god, Bes was often shown with grotesque features and a protruding tongue.

Lotus flower

Horus
This magical stela was intended to protect a family from the natural dangers of living in Egypt. The god Horus (often shown as a child) stands on the backs of crocodiles, preventing them from snatching any members of the family. In his hands he grips dangers found in the deserts, such as snakes, scorpions, lions, and gazelles, which were sometimes thought to be creatures of ill omen.

Temples

The temples of ancient Egypt were run by high-ranking priests who performed duties on behalf of the pharaoh. Chief priests had great wealth and power—they controlled all the temple treasuries and vast estates. The office of chief priest was often held by one family for generations, until a pharaoh appointed an outsider. Lower-ranking priests served in the temple, kept records, and looked after temple property.

Feed the birds
Symbols of the god Thoth, ibises were sacred in Egypt. This 19th-century painting shows ibises being fed by a priestess.

Sidelock of hair

Kneeling priest
This type of priest was called a "Yun-mutef" priest, meaning "Pillar of his Mother." He symbolizes the god Horus as a child. His hair is in a sidelock to represent youth.

Offering table

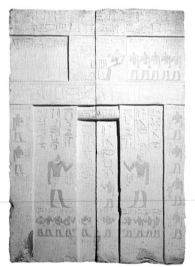

False door
Courtiers had tomb chapels with false doors that represented a point of contact between the living and the dead. "Soul priests" would leave offerings of food and drink at these doors. On this door, several priests are shown bringing meat, poultry, and bread to the tomb.

Paw and tail of leopardskin

The Temple of Dendera
The goddess Hathor's temple as it survives today dates from the time when Egypt was ruled by Greeks and Romans (see pp. 62–63).

Last of the temples

This painting by 19th-century artist David Roberts shows the temple of Isis on the island of Philae. This was the last Egyptian temple to fall to the Christians. It later became a church.

Colossal carvings

Ramesses II ordered two temples to be carved in the cliffs at Abu Simbel in Nubia. This one was carved for himself and three Egyptian gods—Amun, Re-Harakhty, and Ptah.

Obelisks

Stone obelisks were carved with the titles of kings and dedications to the gods. The pointed tip of the obelisk represents the ground on which the Sun-god stood to create the universe.

Gatepost

This obelisk was one of two that stood at the entrance of the temple at Luxor. The other obelisk is now in the Place de la Concorde, Paris.

Thinker

The lines on this priest's forehead and the wide open stare are meant to show that he is a serious thinker. He is bald because most Egyptian priests had to shave their hair.

Winged sky goddess

Son of Horus, who looked after mummified body of priestess

Golden coffin

This coffin, made of gilded wood, belonged to a priestess who served the god Amun. Her face is carved in the way she would like to look for eternity.

Sacred rituals

Sacred bucket
This bronze container, called a situla, held holy water from the sacred lake of the temple. It would have been used in ceremonies involving the sprinkling of holy water.

Only very high-ranking priests were allowed in the temple sanctuary. Bearing incense and holy water, the high priest would break the seal on the door of the shrine that held a gold statue of the god. The priests then decorated the statue and made an offering of food. As they went out, one of the priests swept the floor so that no trace of their presence was left behind.

Crescent and full Moons worshiped by baboons

Ritual vase
Sacred water held in metal vases was poured over offering tables to show the purity of the offering. The vases also held a mixture of water and natron (see p. 15) used for ritual washing.

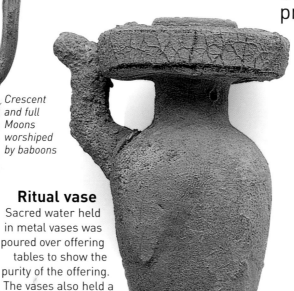

Worshiper
This priestess, a woman named Deniu-en-Khons, is making offerings to the god Re-Harakhty. He is holding the ankh, the Egyptian sign of life.

Cup in which incense was burned

Container for pellets of incense

Tapered base allowing situla to rest on a stand

Procession

These priests have shaved their hair to ensure cleanliness. Their leader carries an incense burner and a vase of sacred water.

Offerings

This plaque shows a priest pouring sacred water over offerings of bread and a vase of liquid. At the front is a channel for the holy water to drain away.

Baboon

Bird

Jackal

Frog

This is one of many temple paintings showing incense burners in use.

Air freshener

Incense burns with an aroma that rises with the smoke. It was used in temples to attract the attention of the god and to purify the air in the temple.

Goddess Mut

Standard finial

Priests carried standards (flags) in temple processions. All that has survived of these are the emblems on top of the supporting poles. This one is topped by the falcon-god Horus, who is identified with the king of Egypt.

Head of Hathor

Khonsu

Cult mirror

Beauty aids, such as mirrors and cosmetic palettes, were placed in temples for the use of the god. On the handle of this example, a crescent rises toward a hawk, symbolizing a Moon god such as Khonsu. Heads of the goddess Hathor adorn the columns on the face of the mirror. The goddess Mut is the figure in the center.

Ivory handle

Scribes

Reading and writing were important skills in ancient Egypt. Official record keepers, known as scribes, held high positions in Egyptian society. One scribe, Horemheb, even became king. The training was thorough—boys had to train for about five years from the age of nine. They learned to carve hieroglyphs (picture symbols) into stone and write on sheets of papyrus with mineral pigments. Once qualified, scribes would be free from paying taxes and doing national service during times of flood.

Ready for work
Scribes were often shown sitting cross-legged with their papyrus.

Hole for ink

Bushy top of plant

Goose census
This scribe is counting geese on a nobleman's estate. He will enter the total number on his scroll for tax records.

Papyrus
This triangular-stemmed reed about 13 ft (4 m) tall grew along the banks of the Nile. It vanished due to overuse for boats, rope, sandals, and writing material.

Stem used for writing material

Outer rind peeled away

Alternate layers

Inner pith cut into strips

Stone

Mallet

Papyrus sheets
Strips of pith were laid in two layers: one vertical, the next horizontal. They were covered with linen and flattened with stones or a mallet. Eventually, the strips would bind together in their own sap.

Grinder for crushing pigments

Art palette
This palette belonged to a royal scribe. His pigments would have been made from red ocher, or blue or green minerals. Black was made from soot or charcoal.

Draftsmen
Scribes called draftsmen were sometimes asked to design royal monuments. Unfinished tombs like that of King Horemheb show the stages involved in designing and painting. First, junior artists drew the scenes in red ocher on dry plaster. Next, senior artists outlined corrections in black. The painters would then fill in the outlines with color.

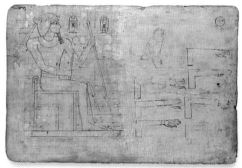

Sketch of Tuthmosis III
The artist drew the figure of the king on a grid to get the right proportions.

Wooden palette
Most scribes had a portable wooden palette like this which they took on their travels.

Scribes and supervisor
These two scribes appear to be writing down the words of their supervisor on their scrolls. A document container stands in front of them.

Name of Ramesses

Reed brushes for precision writing

Sign for scribe
This hieroglyphic sign shows a brush holder, a water pot, and a palette, together making up the Egyptian word for a scribe.

Brushes
The thick brush made of papyrus twine would have been used to paint large walls. The smaller one was probably used to paint hieroglyphs on statues.

Writing

Scribes had to be experts in writing hieroglyphs, a form of picture-writing with about 700 different signs. Hieroglyphs were used on tombs, monuments, and in religious texts. The hieratic script was a faster version of hieroglyphs and was used for everyday purposes. Later, the simpler demotic script was used to write legal documents. At the end of Egyptian civilization, scribes had to be able to write Greek, the language of their overlords.

Label
Scribes used tags like this to label their scrolls. This tag dates from the reign of Amenhotep III.

Two scripts
Scribes usually used the faster hieratic script to write on papyrus (above, left). Hieroglyphs are used above the figures.

Imhotep
This talented scribe lived 4,500 years ago. He was a high priest of the Sun-god, as well as being the designer of the first pyramid at Saqqara.

Royal door plate
This metal plate reads: "There shall always exist the Son of Re whom he loves, Amenhotep the god, ruler of Thebes."

King's name contained in oval border called a cartouche

Cylinder seal
This seal bears the name of King Meryre and one of his officials. To the right is the impression showing the complete surface of the seal.

Cartouche bearing name of King Meryre

Name of Meryre's official

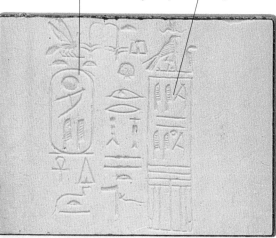

Top Underside Small scarab

The Rosetta Stone

When the last temple was closed in the sixth century CE, the ability to read hieroglyphs was lost until this stone was discovered in 1799. On the stone are three scripts. The bottom section is in Greek, the center in demotic, and the top is in hieroglyphs. The three scripts contained the same text, so by reading the Greek script archeologists could translate the other two and decipher the hieroglyphs.

Scarab seal

Stamp seals included names, titles, or information that the owner would stamp on clay or papyrus. This scarab seal tells us that Amenhotep III killed 102 lions during his reign.

Hieroglyphs

Scribes chose pictures for their script from the world around them. The barn owl represented the consonant "m." On the carving in the picture it forms part of the royal name "Amen em hat."

Translator

The Rosetta Stone was found at Rosetta in the western Delta. After many years of study, French scholar Jean-François Champollion finally deciphered it in 1822.

Deciphering the stone

As the stone contained royal names, such as Ptolemy, their equivalents could be found in the hieroglyphs at the top. From this, the hieroglyphs making other words could be gradually deciphered.

Notebook

Some hieroglyphic signs needed a lot of practice from pupil scribes. Here a scribe has been practicing the duckling hieroglyph, which was used in writing the word for "prime minister."

Weapons of war

The Egyptian army was well organized. Led by the pharaoh, the army consisted of groups of 50 soldiers, including archers, spearmen, and charioteers. Egyptian chariots were pulled by horses and acted as platforms from which archers could fire at the enemy. Scribes also went to war to keep records of the campaigns. In peacetime, soldiers performed civil duties, such as digging irrigation canals or building pyramids.

Soldiers carrying weapons are following orders given by trumpet

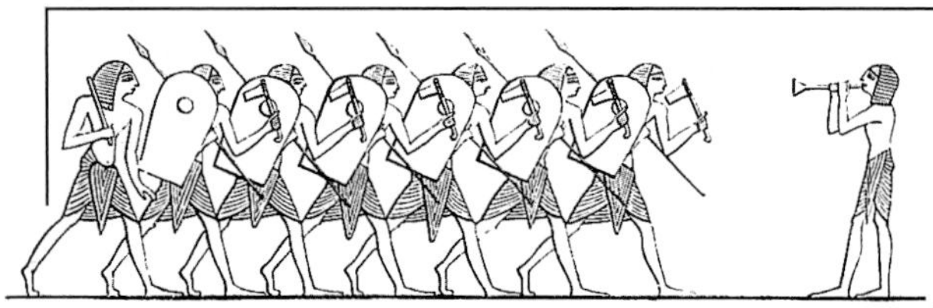

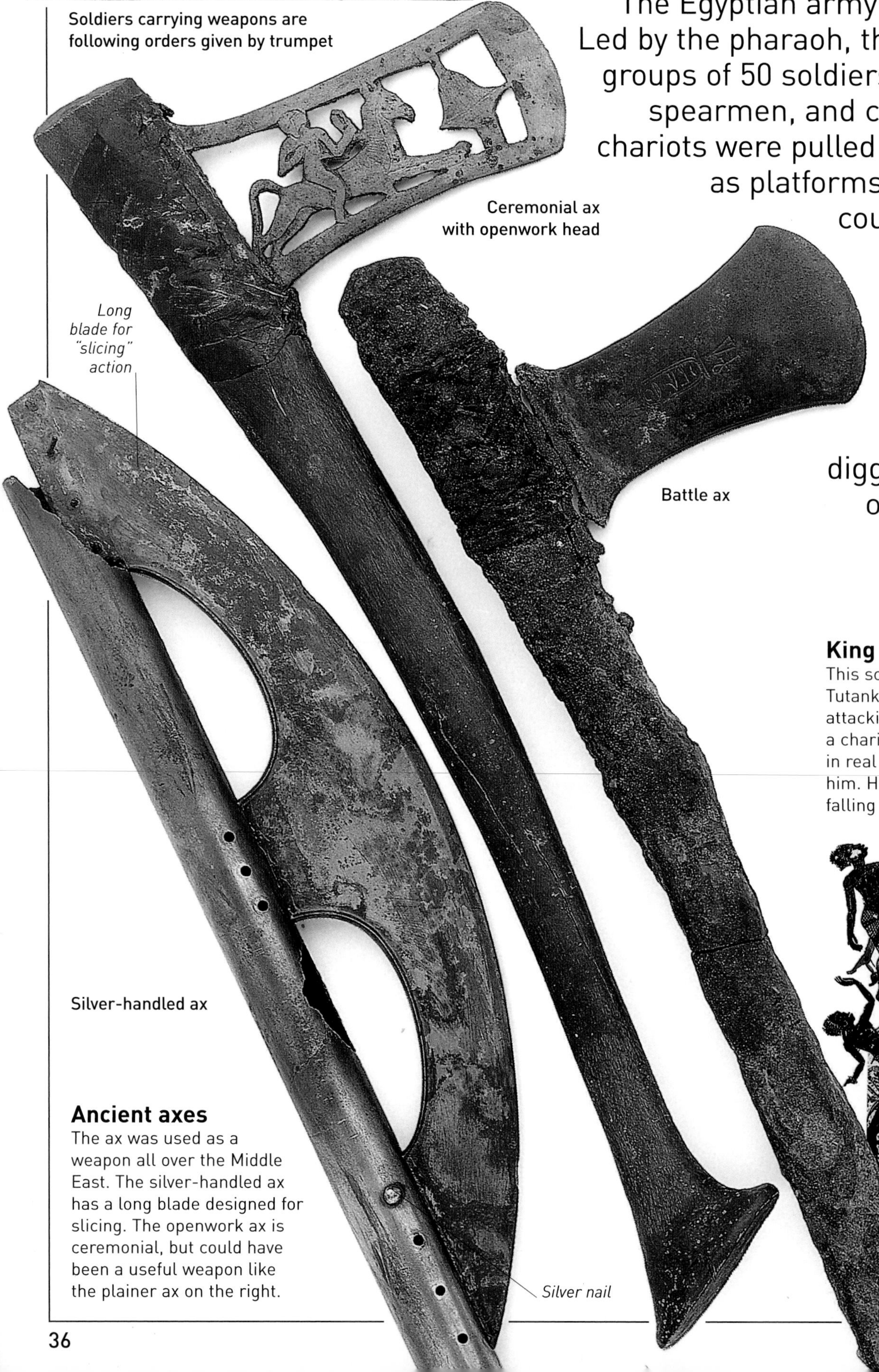

Ceremonial ax with openwork head

Long blade for "slicing" action

Battle ax

Silver-handled ax

Silver nail

Ancient axes

The ax was used as a weapon all over the Middle East. The silver-handled ax has a long blade designed for slicing. The openwork ax is ceremonial, but could have been a useful weapon like the plainer ax on the right.

King at war

This scene from a box discovered in Tutankhamun's tomb shows the king attacking the Nubians. He rides alone in a chariot drawn by two horses, although in real life a charioteer would have driven him. His enemies are falling in disarray.

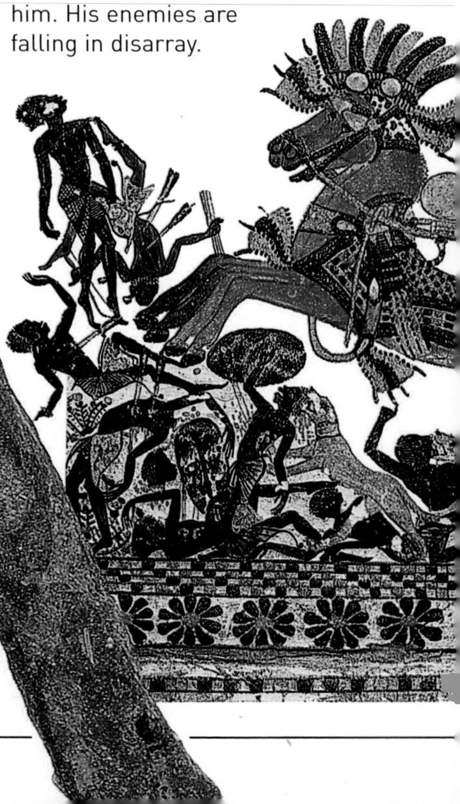

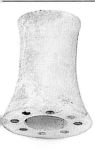

Flint
heads

Finger guard
This bone guard protected an archer's finger from the pain caused by pulling the bow string taut.

Small but deadly
Egyptian arrowheads were made of bronze. The horseshoe shapes were meant to wound, while the triangular arrowheads were designed to kill.

Bronze
heads

Trusty blades
With straighter handles than daggers, swords were influenced by designs from the Middle East. They could be gripped tightly and fitted with longer blades.

Arrow
With its blunt tip and reed shaft, this may have been a hunter's weapon.

Dagger

Medals
Gold flies were given to those who had fought bravely.

Deadly dagger
Egyptian daggers had finely tapered copper blades. The bone or ivory handles fit into the palm of the hand. Soldiers carried their daggers either openly in their belts or in wooden sheaths.

On the march
These foot soldiers are armed with battle axes, spears, and large wooden shields.

Tutankhamun wears a wrist protector

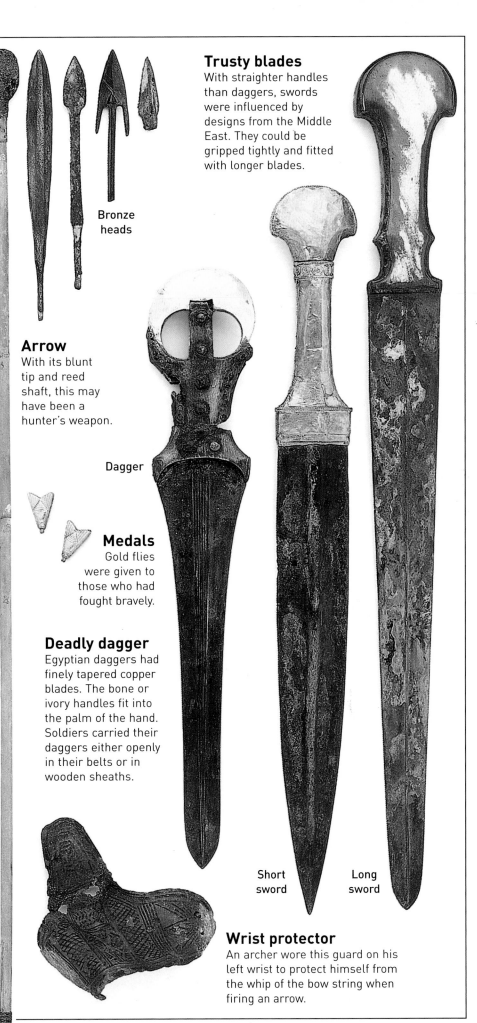

Short
sword

Long
sword

Wrist protector
An archer wore this guard on his left wrist to protect himself from the whip of the bow string when firing an arrow.

Sailing on the Nile

The Nile River was Egypt's main highway. Boats were used for transporting everything from grain and cattle to blocks of granite taken from quarries. Ceremonial ships made of cedar wood were used to transport state officials and the pharaoh's coffin. In 1954, a boat made for King Khufu was discovered in a pit next to the Great Pyramid (see pp. 20–21). Built around 4,500 years ago, the ceremonial barge was 142 ft (43 m) long and was probably intended for Khufu's journey with the Sun-god in the afterlife.

The Ra expedition
Early boats were made of papyrus. Later, they were built from wood. Explorer Thor Heyerdhal sailed his papyrus ship, "Ra," from Egypt to the US, showing that a papyrus boat could survive an ocean crossing.

Gone fishing
These skiffs are made of bundles of papyrus reeds tied together with twine. They are propelled by two oarsmen and are linked by a net edged with floats. The fishermen have already made a catch.

Ox-hide canopy

Steering oar

Steersman

Dhow
In the 19th century, dhows were as common on the Nile as they were in ancient times.

Work in progress
A small boat is propped up with logs while the shipwrights are bending planks by twisting the ropes with sticks. Other workers are hammering nails into holes and planing the support for the steering oar.

Cedars
Cedar and juniper trees, used for building grand ceremonial boats, grew on the hills of Lebanon and Syria. King Sneferu sent 40 boats to Byblos to collect cedar wood. Cedar trees grew 65 –108 ft (20–33 m), and gave the largest lumber for the biggest boats.

Square sail

Men pulling sail into breeze

All aboard
The measure of wealth for a landowner was the number of cattle he owned. Transporting cattle across the Nile could be difficult because the water was too deep for wading. So special broad vessels were made for cows. Here, the animals are shown balancing precariously on top of the deck stalls. In reality, they would have been standing on the deck.

Men pushing boat off sandbank

Tomb boat
Model boats like this one from 4,000 years ago were put in tombs as transportation for the afterlife. Here, some of the men are fixing the sail in position, while others lean on poles to push the boat away from the shore. At the bow, a sailor is testing the depth of the water with a plumbline. The boat's owner sits beneath the canopy.

Plumbline to test depth of water

Buying and selling

Bartering
This was a common way of buying goods. Items such as ducks or wine could be exchanged for goods of a similar value.

Egypt was the wealthiest country of the ancient world. Pharaohs would send gold from Egyptian mines as gifts to foreign rulers and receive manufactured goods in return. Traders traveled to Nubia, an area south of the Nile, to exchange goods such as crops and minerals for luxury items, including panther skins, ivory tusks, and lions for the temples.

Rates of exchange
Goods were valued according to a standard weight of copper called a "deben." For example, a bed was worth 2.5 deben. This piece of stone lists items sold by an man named Amenwau.

4 deben

5 kite

2 kite

1 kite

Weighing it up
The "deben" originally weighed around 0.5 oz (14 g). Later, it was revalued at 3 oz (91 g), divided into 10 "kite."

Hoard of silver
These pieces of silver were buried in a pot at El-Amarna. Because the value of metal was measured by its weight, the shape of the pieces was unimportant.

Large balance for weighing produce

Unloading pottery wine jars from a Nile boat belonging to a high official

Ivory spoon
Elephant tusks, traded in Nubia, were made into luxury items, such as this spoon carved with the head of the goddess Hathor. If ivory from Nubia was in short supply, the teeth of hippos could be used instead.

Cassia
Dried laurel bark called cassia was brought from India. It was used for perfume and incense.

The land of Punt
The unknown land of Punt was seen as a remote and exotic place. To reach it, merchants sailed along the coast of the Red Sea, then inland toward the Atbara River. In the 15th century BCE, Queen Hatshepsut sent five boats to Punt. After landing in eastern Sudan they were taken inland, where they saw people living in houses on stilts to protect them from wild animals. The main cargo brought back from Punt was incense.

Frankincense
This fragrant gum resin came from trees in Somalia, Yemen, and Sudan.

Ivory fittings

Ebony handle

Hathor has the ears of the cow, her sacred animal

Syrian gifts
These Syrian princes are bringing gifts of gold vases and perfume holders to the pharaoh. One prince brings his daughter to be brought up at court.

Fly whisk
Ebony, the wood used to make this fly whisk, was imported from central Africa via Nubia.

Lapis lazuli bull set in gold

Lapis lazuli
Merchants from Afghanistan brought this valuable stone to trading centers like Byblos in Lebanon.

Unworked lapis lazuli

The incense trade
Traders brought myrrh and frankincense from Punt. In addition to the resin, they took whole trees to plant in front of Queen Hatshepsut's temple.

Kingly carving
This miniature figure of the mummified Tutankhamun is expertly carved. The king, wearing his royal headcloth, lies between the hawk god and a human-headed bird that represents his soul.

Tools

Egyptian carpenters had access to a variety of lumber in the Nile valley. Local woods included the date palm used for roofing beams, the acacia for pegs and dowels, and the sycamore fig for coffins, chests, and tables. Highly prized woods, such as cedar and ebony, were imported from Lebanon, Syria, and Africa to make furniture and statues. Egyptian carpenters were highly skilled and often held well-paid jobs. Many of their tools have survived to the present day.

Figurine
This elaborate cosmetic container is delicately carved in the shape of a Nubian servant girl.

Serrated metal blade

Metal blade bound with leather

Wooden shaft

Chopper
The ax appears in the hieroglyph for the word for carpenter. Axes were mainly used to cut down trees and to hack wood roughly into shape.

Saw
Egyptian saws were pulled through wood, unlike modern saws, which are pushed and pulled. Tomb scenes show carpenters using saws like this.

Headrest
Egyptians relaxed with their heads supported by a pillow resting on a wooden stand. Air could circulate below the neck, and the head was raised to avoid contact with insects or scorpions. This headrest is in the shape of a desert hare.

Adze
This tool was used for planing surfaces such as boat hulls to a smooth finish. It was also used to carve large funerary chests.

Goat's head

Chairs, boxes, and chests were often decorated with animal features. A chair could have legs in the shape of a lion's paws, or carved snakes sitting on its arms. The small fragment on the right has been exquisitely carved to show the horn, curly fleece, and beard of a goat.

Men at work

These carpenters are working on a casket that has been inlaid with colorful materials. One hammers out a hole for a peg while the other polishes the lid.

Hare's ears support pillow and head

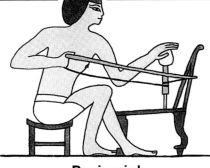

Boring job

To bore a hole in a plank the carpenter used a drill consisting of a metal point in a wooden shaft. He placed the drill where he wanted the hole to be and rotated the cutting edge with a bow.

Bradawl

A bradawl made "starter holes" so that the drill could grip. It also made marks to show where the pegs would go.

Chisel

Carpenters used chisels for intricate carving and for cutting hieroglyphs into wooden surfaces.

Twine

Wooden bow

Metal drill bit

Smoothing stone

The rough surfaces left after carving could be smoothed down using a pebble. Pebbles were also used to give furniture a highly polished finish.

Drill

Carpenters used a bow-drill to make holes for the pegs that joined pieces of wood together. This bow-drill is well-worn.

Hunting and fishing

Farming produced more food than people needed in ancient Egypt, so hunting was mainly done for sport. The king and his courtiers went to the deserts to hunt wild bulls, antelopes, and lions. The bulls would be herded into an enclosure and picked off one by one by the pharaoh in his chariot. Fish from the Nile were usually caught in nets or with hooks. Bird hunting was also popular. The hunter would use a boat to approach the papyrus reeds where the wildfowl were resting. When the birds flew up in the air, he would hurl a throwstick at them.

Family outing
This nobleman is using a snake-shaped throwstick to hunt birds in the papyrus marshes. Accompanying him on the trip are his wife, daughter, and cat, which has already caught three birds.

Arrows
Egyptian arrows were made of reeds and were tipped with ivory, bone, flint, obsidian, or metal.

Flat tips to weaken animal by piercing hide

Sharp tip to kill outright

Cleft end for bow string

Hippos
The hippo could cause havoc among boats on the Nile. So teams of men would go to hunt hippos, gradually weakening them by repeated spearing until they collapsed.

Throwstick
Shaped like boomerangs, wooden throwsticks were hurled at birds to kill or stun them.

Desert spoils

Desert hares are often shown in Egyptian hunting scenes. Antelopes and gazelles were also found in the desert, and ostrich eggs were a desert delicacy.

Hooks

Fish were caught by copper or bronze hooks, then gutted and dried in the sun.

Weights

Like fishermen today, the Egyptians used lead weights to keep their fishing nets under the water.

Fishing net

Nets made from reed and papyrus twine were designed to trap both birds and fish. They were kept in position by reed-floats. This net on the right is about 3,000 years old.

Courtiers used this type of harpoon to test their skill.

Prong to attach rope

Harpoons

Metal harpoons were used to catch fish and large game, such as the hippo. In ancient Egypt, the hippo was associated with the god Seth, who caused chaos.

In the home

Houses in ancient Egypt were built from sun-dried mud bricks. The mud was strengthened with a mixture of straw and pebbles then molded in wooden frames. The walls of the houses were covered with plaster and the insides were often painted with scenes from nature. Windows were small to keep out the heat. Wealthy families had large houses that contained a hall, a kitchen, several bedrooms, and stairs leading up to the roof.

Around the pool
Wealthy families often had a pool in the yard that was stocked with lotuses and fish. The water was changed regularly to keep it fresh.

Home comforts
This home belonged to a successful official, the royal scribe Nakht. Grille windows high on the walls kept out light and dust, while vents trapped the cool north wind. There would also have been a garden and a pool.

Soul house
This model shows the house of a poorer family. The model, known as a "soul house," would have been placed in the tomb of the owner for use in the afterlife. The entrance is a low, arched doorway and models of food items, have been placed in the walled courtyard.

Roof terrace

Empty vessels

A variety of Egyptian cups, jars, and pots still survive today. Among the earliest are stoneware vessels, made over 5,000 years ago from mottled stone. Later, potters used a material called faience, made by heating up powdered quartz in a mold. Some Egyptian jars had pointed bases because they were designed to rest on stands.

Drinking cup
Water, wine, or beer could have been drunk from this beautiful faience cup decorated with a lotus-flower pattern.

Wine jar
This wine jar was made in about 1000 BCE. It is made of faience and is decorated with diamond and leaf patterns.

Bird in hand
Carved over 5,000 years ago from a stone called breccia, this vase was used to store oil or other liquids.

Fruit basket
Baskets were made from palm leaves or strips of papyrus. They were often used as household containers—this one holds two dom palm fruit.

Offerings for the deceased

Fanning the fire
This servant is fanning charcoal to make a fire. The fire provided both heat for cooking and a warm place for servants to gather and talk.

These Egyptian chairs look graceful from the side

Food and drink

Butchers at work
This model shows an ox being slaughtered for food.

The rich mud deposited by the Nile flood allowed farmers to grow barley and wheat, which were used to make bread and beer. Farmers also grew vegetables, such as leeks, lentils, and lettuce, and fruits, such as gourds, figs, and melons. Grapes from the Nile Delta were made into wine or dried into raisins. The wealthy enjoyed lavish banquets where courses of duck, gazelle, or roasted ox were followed by cakes sweetened with honey or dates. Poorer people would have eaten less meat and poultry and more fish.

In the vineyard
Two men pluck bunches of grapes from the vines to make wine. They would then crush the grapes by stepping on them.

Bread
More than 3,000 years old, this bread was baked from barley dough. Its texture is tough—grit sometimes got in the flour during grinding.

Strainer
Made from mashed loaves of barley-bread, Egyptian beer was very thick and had to be strained through a basket or with a wooden syphon.

Perforations for straining

A Syrian soldier serving the pharaoh Akhenaten shown drinking beer through a siphon

Grapes
Most grapes grew in the north of Egypt. Both red and green grapes provided the fermented juice for wine.

Delicious dates

Dates were eaten fresh at harvest time in August or could be dried in a sweet mash. The sap from dates was also used to make wine.

Sycamore figs

The fruit of the sycamore fig was highly prized in ancient Egypt. Baboons loved figs and are often shown helping themselves from bowls or straight from the trees.

Modern fig

Palm-tree fruit

These dom palm fruit come from a 3,000-year-old tomb offering. The outer case is so tough it could be used as the top end of a drill.

Large pomegranate produced by modern agriculture

Egyptian banquet

Scribes and nobles enjoyed a wide variety of meat, poultry, and fruit, as shown in this Theban banquet scene. The courses included cakes, figs, grapes, the head of a calf, the heart and leg of an ox, a goose, and a twist of onions.

Pomegranates

The pomegranate was introduced to Egypt from the Middle East. Its skin may have been used to produce a yellowish dye. This dish contains fruits that were once part of a tomb offering.

Ancient fruit

Song and dance

The Egyptians enjoyed life to the full. At large public festivals, people were entertained by singing, dancing, and music from flutes, harps, and castanets. Music was also part of everyday life. Farmers would sing to their oxen to make them work better, and winemakers crushed their grapes to the sound of rhythm sticks being clapped together. No one knows what Egyptian music sounded like, but an orchestra at a banquet was likely to have included string, wind, and percussion sections.

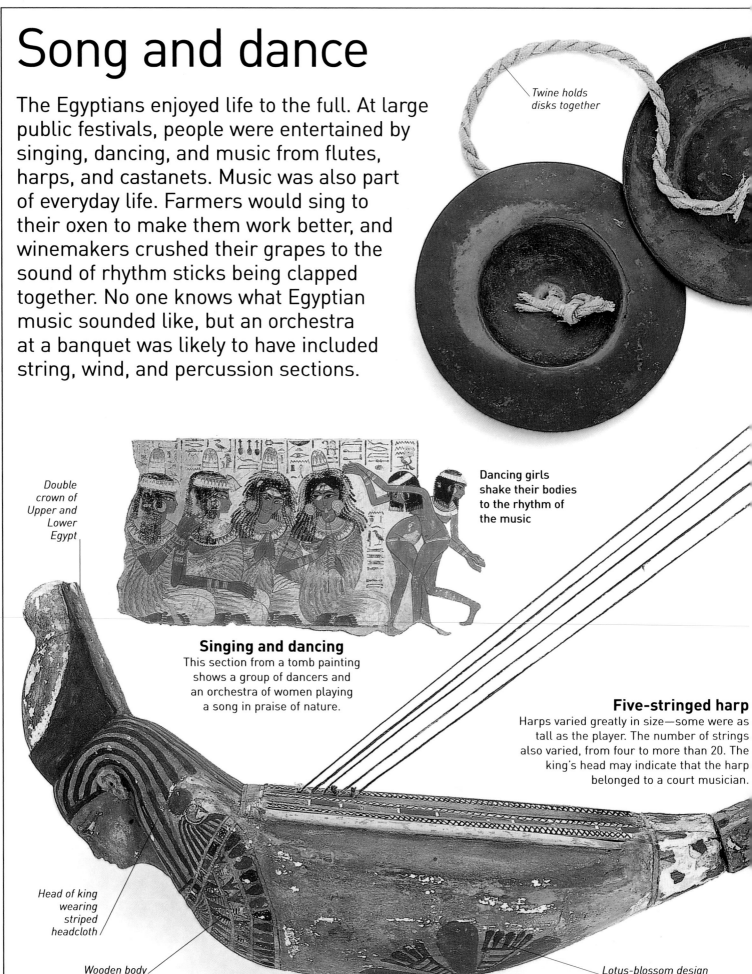

Twine holds disks together

Double crown of Upper and Lower Egypt

Dancing girls shake their bodies to the rhythm of the music

Singing and dancing
This section from a tomb painting shows a group of dancers and an orchestra of women playing a song in praise of nature.

Five-stringed harp
Harps varied greatly in size—some were as tall as the player. The number of strings also varied, from four to more than 20. The king's head may indicate that the harp belonged to a court musician.

Head of king wearing striped headcloth

Wooden body

Lotus-blossom design

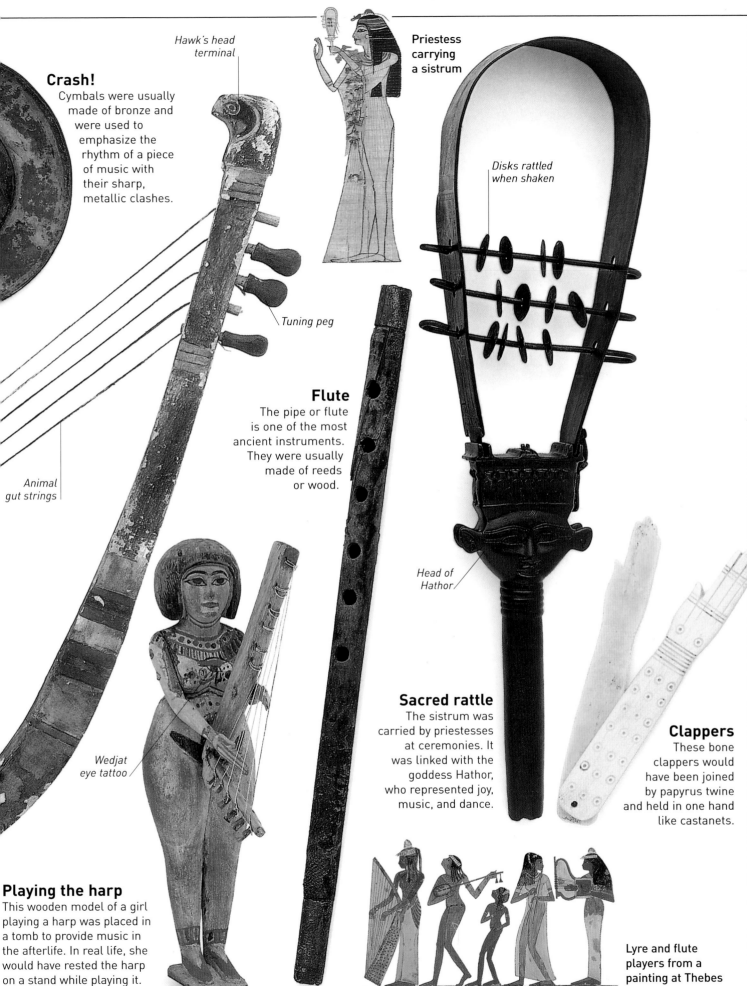

Crash!

Cymbals were usually made of bronze and were used to emphasize the rhythm of a piece of music with their sharp, metallic clashes.

Hawk's head terminal

Tuning peg

Animal gut strings

Priestess carrying a sistrum

Disks rattled when shaken

Flute

The pipe or flute is one of the most ancient instruments. They were usually made of reeds or wood.

Head of Hathor

Sacred rattle

The sistrum was carried by priestesses at ceremonies. It was linked with the goddess Hathor, who represented joy, music, and dance.

Clappers

These bone clappers would have been joined by papyrus twine and held in one hand like castanets.

Wedjat eye tattoo

Playing the harp

This wooden model of a girl playing a harp was placed in a tomb to provide music in the afterlife. In real life, she would have rested the harp on a stand while playing it.

Lyre and flute players from a painting at Thebes

This carved lion head was used as a counter

Games

Egyptian children played with balls, dolls, and wooden toys, just as children do today. They also played leapfrog, jacks, and tug-of-war. Adults preferred board games, such as snake and the more complicated senet. The Egyptians were great storytellers and kept their children amused with tales of imagination and enchantment.

Clay balls
These colorful clay balls were originally filled with seeds or clay beads so that they rattled as they were thrown.

Wooden doll
This wooden doll has hair made of clay beads attached to twine. It may have been a toy or it could have been put in a tomb as company for the afterlife.

Ball games
A popular pastime was throwing and catching balls. Sometimes this was played on piggyback.

Horse on wheels
Horse-riding was a favorite pastime of the pharaohs. This toy horse has a saddle mat thrown over it. It was pulled along by a rope through the muzzle.

Twine to move lower jaw

Toy mouse
The tail of this mouse moved up and down.

Wooden cat
This toy is carved roughly into a catlike shape. Its jaw opens and closes when the string is pulled.

Senet

This board game symbolized a struggle against the forces of evil that tried to prevent a person from reaching the kingdom of the god Osiris. There were two sets of counters and 30 squares on the board. Some of the squares were dangerous to land on; others were lucky.

Spinning tops
These tops were made of powdered quartz formed in a mold and then glazed. A vigorous twist of the fingers or a tug on the papyrus twine that was wound around the cone would set them spinning.

Your move
This papyrus shows the scribe Ani playing senet with his wife, Tutu. The artist has shown Tutu sitting behind her husband in a formal pose.

Fit for a king
Tutankhamun's tomb contained four senet boards, including this fine ebony and ivory one. It has a special drawer for the counters.

Hieroglyph of pharaoh's name

Stone ball used in the snake game

Snake game
One of the earliest board games found in Egypt was called "snake." The stone board represented a coiled serpent. The winner would be the first to move his or her counter around the squares to the middle. The counters were sometimes carved with the names of pharaohs.

Clothes and cloth

From early times, people in Egypt wore simple clothes made of linen. The cloth was woven from the fibers of a flowering plant called flax, which was widely cultivated in Egypt. Most Egyptian men wore short skirts called kilts, which were tied in a knot at the waist. Women wore long, tight-fitting dresses under beautifully pleated cloaks. The Egyptians had clever ways of protecting their clothes—soldiers covered the backs of their kilts with leather netting and servants wore beaded nets over their dresses. The Egyptians learned how to dye their clothes in colored patterns from the Middle East, but the technique was never widespread.

Man and wife
Both men and women wore braided wigs in ancient Egypt.

Leather sandals
These sandals are made from pieces of ox leather sewn with papyrus twine. Leather was rarely used for footwear in Egypt.

Reinforced edge

Reed sandals
Papyrus and other reeds were the most common materials for sandals. Egyptian priests were forbidden to wear any other material on their feet.

Twine securing strap

Wigs
The courtiers on this wall relief are wearing typical wigs. Egyptian wigs were made of human hair and stuck in place with beeswax.

Royal statue

This statue dates from the reign of Akhenaten (see p. 10). It could be a statue of Nefertiti (Akhenaten's queen) or one of her daughters. She is shown wearing a very fine, pleated garment of royal linen.

In the groove

This board was used for pleating linen. The damp cloth would be pressed into the grooves.

Flax comb

The heads of the flax fibers were removed with a long comb. Then the stems were soaked, beaten, and combed again to prepare them for spinning.

Linen sheet

Types of linen in Egypt ranged from coarse cloth like this to the finest gauze worn by royalty.

Spindle

The flax fibers were spun on sticks called spindles, which were weighted down by a stone wheel, or whorl.

Spinner

This girl is drawing out the twisted fibers, which are attached to the rotating spindle.

All that glitters

Egyptian mines between the Nile and the Red Sea coast contained vast quantities of gold. This precious metal was either beaten into shape or cast in molds. Egyptian jewelers also had access to semiprecious stones from the deserts, such as the orange-red carnelian, green feldspar, and mauve amethyst. Some stones were imported from abroad— turquoise came from the Sinai peninsula and rich blue lapis lazuli came from Afghanistan.

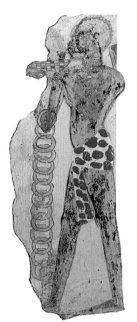

Rings of gold being brought to Egypt from Nubia

Bracelet

Made for Prince Nemareth, this bracelet shows the god Horus as a child (see p. 27). Like many children in Egyptian art, he is shown sucking his finger.

Hieroglyphs give name of owner

Cowrie shell shows wish of wearer to have children

Lucky girdle

This girdle, or belt, contains lucky charms made of electrum (a mixture of gold and silver) and beads of carnelian, amethyst, lapis lazuli, and turquoise.

A star is born

This star was worn on a headdress called a diadem. This painting shows a Roman priest wearing a similar diadem.

Gold diadem

Ear ornaments

Many Egyptians had pierced ears. The holes in the ear lobes would have needed to be fairly large for these studs.

Gold earrings

Faience stud

Glass stud

Jasper stud

Falcon pectoral

A pectoral was a type of jewelery worn on the chest. The frame of this falcon was originally filled with pieces of faience, glass, and gems.

Metal strips bent into shape and soldered on to base

Talon holds the "shenu" symbol, meaning eternity

Traces of original inlay

Jewelers at work

Many objects were made by heating metal until it was liquid, then pouring it into molds.

Gift of a king

Outstanding service to the state was rewarded by gifts of jewelery. The king would drop collars or bracelets from a window to nobles waiting below. This collar has three rows of gold rings threaded together on twine.

Finger rings

Rings often contained a swiveling stone in the shape of a scarab beetle (see p. 24). These scarabs are made of steatite that was easy to carve.

Scarab

Steatite and gold ring

Steatite and gold ring

Silver ring

Fish amulets, to prevent drowning

Hair worn in a sidelock represented youth

Heh, the god of "millions of years," symbolizes long life

Beards or sidelocks of youth

Body beautiful

Malachite

Beauty and fashion were very important to the Egyptians. They went to great lengths to adorn themselves with cosmetics, wigs, floral garlands, and fine linen. Both men and women used eye paint made from minerals crushed on fine slate palettes. Many of their beauty aids, including combs, mirrors, and cosmetic holders, have survived to the present day.

Tube with royal inscription

Applicators
These were used for scooping, mixing, and applying pigments.

Containers
Ground minerals for eye paint were mixed with water and kept in tubes like these.

Craftsman's masterpiece
The mother duck's back wings slide across to give access to the face cream inside.

Perfume pomades
Wigs would often be topped with cones of scented animal fat, which melted slowly.

Pot made of the rare stone anhydrite

Mirror

Courtiers used mirrors made of polished bronze or copper. Royal mirrors were made of silver.

Galena

Polished metal reflective surface

Iron oxide

Pigments

The Egyptians made green eye paint from malachite, a copper ore. A lead ore known as galena produced black eye paint ("kohl"). Cheeks and lips could be reddened with ochers made from iron minerals. Fat would usually be added to the makeup to help its application.

Floral spoon

The handle of this container represents a bunch of flowers. The top swivels to reveal the cosmetic inside.

Fragrant massage

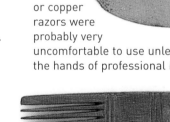

This noblewoman is having water poured over her while being massaged. A friend holds a flower for her to smell.

Tweezers

Hair

Priests and women used tweezers to remove hair. Tongs were used to curl the hair.

Hair curler

Double ends for different sized curls

Razors

Bronze or copper razors were probably very uncomfortable to use unless in the hands of professional barbers.

Wooden comb

Egyptians combed their wigs with ivory and wooden combs. Wigs were often long and heavy, with up to three layers of curls.

Touching up

Here a noblewoman called Ipwet uses a mirror to dab powder on her cheeks.

Hairpins

These were used to keep curls or perfume pomades in place.

Birds and beasts

Ancient Egypt was home to a wide range of animals. Lions, wild bulls, and gazelles roamed the deserts. Birds, including pintail ducks and pelicans, built their nests in the papyrus thickets by the Nile. Crocodiles lurked on the riverbanks, and in the water, catfish and perch darted around the hippos. Animals were thought of as the earthly versions of many gods in ancient Egypt, and their images often appear on sacred objects.

Lion
The lion represented strength and power, and so became a symbol of the king himself.

Peek-a-boo
The goddess Hathor was often portrayed as a cow in the papyrus marshes.

Wild sheep and cat
On this container, a wild sheep is stepping over a cat. Rams symbolized some of the most important gods in ancient Egypt. A curly horned ram could represent Amun-Re, king of the gods.

Animal antics
In this humorous papyrus scene, two enemies—the antelope and the lion—are enjoying a game of senet (see p. 53). A jackal playing a double flute escorts a herd of goats, while a cat lovingly attends to some geese.

Crown of Osiris, made up of ram horns, reeds, and ostrich feathers

Crocodiles
The crocodile was the symbol of the god Sobek. Priests used to keep sacred crocodiles in the temples and decorate them with jewelry and mummify them when they died.

Hippos
The male hippo was seen as an evil omen because of its links with the god Seth, archenemy of Osiris and Horus, rightful rulers of Egypt. Hippos could easily overturn papyrus boats and were often hunted for this reason.

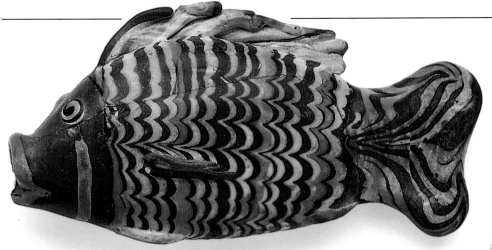

Fish flask

This glass bulti fish was made by molding the glass over a core. The ripples are meant to indicate the fish's scales. The flask was designed to hold perfume, which was poured out of the mouth into the owner's hand.

Geese on parade

These geese are part of a very early tomb painting and were meant to ensure that food in the afterlife would not run out.

Puzzled cat

Cats sacred to the goddess Bastet (see p. 25) were mummified when they died. Their faces were painted to make them look bewildered or silly. They were sold to temple visitors, who took them to the burial grounds and dedicated them to Bastet.

Water plant designs show hippo's aquatic habitat

Small faience hippo

After the pharaohs

Egypt was invaded by foreigners several times in the last 1,000 years BCE. The invaders included the Sudanese, the Persians, and the Macedonians under Alexander the Great. In 30 BCE, Egypt passed into Roman hands. The Arab invasion of the seventh century CE turned Egypt into the mainly Muslim country that it is today.

Cleopatra
Cleopatra VII was the last Greek ruler of Egypt. Her suicide was famous, but there is no evidence to show that she died of a snake bite.

The Romans

The Romans built many temples in Egypt. Although they worshiped Roman gods and goddesses, their emperors were shown on temple walls wearing elaborate Egyptian crowns, and their names were written in hieroglyphs, just like the pharaohs.

Emperor as Horus
Roman emperors were sometimes portrayed as a hawk-headed god, similar to the Egyptian god Horus (see p. 27).

Mummy of Artemidorus

Roman child's mummy

Roman mummies
Mummies of the Roman period often had lifelike portraits of the dead person painted on the coffin. Artemidorus (above) is brightly painted in typical Roman style. These portraits were meant to help the dead person's spirit identify the body to which it belonged.

The Christians

Although there were Christian hermits living in caves before, Egypt officially turned to Christianity with the conversion of the Roman Empire in 324 CE. This version of Christianity was called Coptic, and it still flourishes in the country today. Recently the relics of St. Mark, who is said to have introduced Christianity into Egypt, were sent back from Venice to Cairo.

Tapestry showing the victorious St. George

Survivor

Qasr Ibrim was a Christian city in Nubia that was stormed by Muslim troops. This silver cross survived the attack.

Warrior saint

The image of the god Horus spearing his rival Seth was adopted by early Christians to portray warrior saints like St. George.

Street scene

Up to the 19th century, the streets of Cairo contained craft stalls running alongside the walls and domes of the mosques.

Brass openwork design

The Muslims

Arab armies conquered Egypt in the seventh century CE. Islam became the state religion, Arabic the official language, and the new city of el-Qahira later became the capital, Cairo. Eventually, Egypt was conquered by the Turks. It was not until the 1960s that the country was again governed by a native Egyptian.

Incense burner

This vessel was made about 1,000 years ago to be used in a mosque. Burning incense was part of the ritual of purity observed by Muslims.

Did you know?

FASCINATING FACTS

Priests performing funeral rituals

Because the rituals of death and preparation for the afterlife were so elaborate in ancient Egypt, we know more about how people died than how they lived their everyday lives.

During embalming, the stomach, intestines, lungs, and liver were removed, but the heart was left in place. It was thought to contain a record of past deeds, and it could therefore determine who would be admitted to the afterlife.

Egyptians believed that the hearts and souls of those who did not pass into the afterlife would be consumed by Ammut, the Devourer of the Dead.

One of Tutankhamun's three mummiform (mummy-shaped) coffins

Pharaohs could have several wives, but only one of them would be queen. Many pharaohs married their sisters to strengthen their dynasty's claim to the throne.

Egyptian gods were thought to have beards, so false beards were worn by pharaohs—even female pharaohs—as a symbol of royalty.

The Great Sphinx was buried to its neck for most of its history; it was not cleared completely until 1926. Because pollution is now eroding its stone body, many conservationists think it was better off covered up.

The soles of pharaohs' sandals were sometimes decorated with drawings of their enemies, who would be crushed underfoot symbolically with every step.

When King Tutankhamun's tomb was discovered in 1922, Egyptian-style makeup, clothing, and jewelry suddenly became the height of fashion. Even interiors and graphic design were inspired by Egypt.

Tomb robbers were sometimes the same men who originally built the tombs. If they were caught, they suffered an excruciating death impaled on a sharp wooden stake.

The need to organize the first settlements along the Nile led to the invention of hieroglyphics, or picture-writing. Recent excavations suggest that these were in use several centuries before the earliest writing in Mesopotamia, which is thought to be the "cradle of civilization."

The extravagant and colorful eye makeup associated with ancient Egypt was worn by men as well as women; it was made from ground minerals mixed with water and stored in tubes.

Cleopatra was Macedonian Greek by birth. Highly educated, she spoke seven languages fluently (including Egyptian), but she usually used Greek for official documents.

False beard is a symbol of royalty

QUESTIONS AND ANSWERS

Q How did we get our information about ancient Egypt?

A Much of our knowledge comes from wall paintings, which show us how people looked and what kind tools they used. Written records tell us about daily life, religion, and government. Everyday objects and treasures from archeological sites also reveal details of life in Egypt.

Q Why did the Egyptians go to so much trouble to preserve their dead as mummies?

A They believed that if a dead person's spirit could recognize its own body, the spirit could reinhabit the body and live forever. For this reason, most of the internal organs were carefully removed and preserved. The brain, however, was scooped out with a long hook pushed up one nostril. Since no one was aware of its importance, it was thrown away.

Hook to extract brain

Embalming knife

Q How was King Tutankhamun's mummy stored in his tomb?

A The mummy itself was inside a huge multilayered container. Three coffins, one fitting inside the other, lay in a stone sarcophagus. This rested inside four boxlike shrines, all extravagantly gilded and decorated.

Q What is the curse of King Tutankhamun?

A The curse was said to declare, "Death comes on wings to he who enters a pharaoh's tomb." Although the curse was an invention, several people linked to the excavation did die within a short space of time. Among these was Lord Carnarvon, one of the archeologists who opened the tomb.

Tomb painting from Thebes c. 1450 BCE

Q Why did the color black represent life rather than death?

A The fertile Nile soil was so rich it was almost black, so the Egyptians saw black as the color of life. Red, which resembled the barren desert, represented bad fortune.

Q How did Egyptian rulers pay for their extravagant buildings?

A Ancient Egypt was very wealthy. It had an abundance of minerals, especially gold and semiprecious stones. Also, Egyptian farmers produced far more crops than the people needed, so they could sell the excess abroad.

Record Breakers

☥ **RECORD REIGN**
The pharaoh Pepy II (2278–2184 BCE) has the longest reign of any ruler in history. He came to the throne at the age of six and ruled for 94 years.

☥ **CHANGELESS SOCIETY**
Ancient Egyptian civilization lasted for over 3,000 years, during which time its culture remained largely unchanged.

☥ **FIRST AMONG NATIONS**
Founded in 3100 BCE by King Narmer (sometimes identified with King Menes), Egypt was the world's first nation-state.

☥ **ANCIENT IMAGE**
The earliest surviving life-sized portrait is the statue of King Djoser (2667–2648 BCE), found in an enclosed chamber attached to his pyramid.

Q What role did women play in ancient Egyptian society?

A Although females tended to take on their husband's status in society, they were equal with men under the law and were allowed to own property, do business, inherit money, get divorced, and even reign as pharaoh. The last pharaoh to rule Egypt before the Romans took control was in fact a woman—the legendary Cleopatra.

Life-sized statue of King Djoser

Gold amulet case

The pharaohs

The ancient Egyptians dated events to a particular year in the reign of a king or pharaoh. Later, the kings were sorted into dynasties, a system that is still used today.

Queen Nefertiti

Early Dynastic Period

c. 3100–2890 BCE		c. 2890–2686 BCE	
1st Dynasty		**2nd Dynasty**	
Narmer	3100	Hetepsekhemwy	2890
Aha	3100	Raneb	2865
Djer	3000	Nynetjer	
Djet	2980	Weneg	
Den	2950	Sened	
Anedjib	2925	Peribsen	2700
Semerkhet	2900	Khasekhemwy	2686
Qaa	2890		

# aka Amenhotep IV	† aka Amenophis
* denotes female pharaoh	‡ aka Sesostris
** aka Thutmose	

First Intermediate Period

c. 2181–2125 BCE	c. 2160–2055 BCE
7th & 8th Dynasties	**9th & 10th Dynasties Herakleopolitan**
During this unstable period of Egyptian history there were many temporary kings. Also, the weakening of central power meant that local dynasties became established.	Kheti Merykare Ity
	11th Dynasty (Thebes only)
	Intef I 2125–2112 Intef II 2112–2063 Intef III 2063–2055

Middle Kingdom

c. 2055–1985 BCE	
11th Dynasty All Egypt	
Montuhotep II	055–2004
Montuhotep III	2004–1992
Montuhotep IV	1992–1985

Montuhotep II

New Kingdom

c. 1550–1295 BCE		c. 1295–1186 BCE		c. 1186–1069 BCE	
18th Dynasty		**19th Dynasty**		**20th Dynasty**	
Ahmose	1550–1525	Ramesses I	1295–1294	Sethnakhte	1186–1184
Amenhotep I †	1525–1504	Seti I	1294–1279	Ramesses III	1184–1153
Tuthmosis I**	1504–1492	Ramesses II	1279–1213	Ramesses IV	1153–1147
Tuthmosis II**	1492–1479	Merneptah	1213–1203	Ramesses V	1147–1143
Tuthmosis III**	1479–1425	Amenmessul	203–1200	Ramesses VI	1143–1136
Hatshepsut*	1473–1458	Seti II	1200–1194	Ramesses VII	1136–1129
Amenhotep II †	1427–1400	Saptah	1194–1188	Ramesses VIII	1129–1126
Tuthmosis IV**	1400–1390	Tawosret*	1188–1186	Ramesses IX	1126–1108
Amenhotep III †	1390–1352			Ramesses X	1108–1099
Akhenaten #	1352–1336			Ramesses XI	1099–1069
Nefertiti					
Smenkhkare*	1338–1336				
Tutankhamun	1336–1327				
Ay	1327–1323				
Horemheb	1323–1295				

Ramesses the Great

Late Period

c. 672–525 BCE		c. 525–359 BCE		c. 404–380 BCE		c. 380–343 BCE	
26th Dynasty		**27th Dynasty (Persian Period 1)**		**28th Dynasty**		**30th Dynasty**	
Nekau I	672–664			Amyrtaios	404–399	Nectanebo I	380–362
Psamtek I	664–610	Cambyses	525–522			Teos	362–360
Nekau II	610–595	Darius I	522–486	**29th Dynasty**		Nectanebo II	360–343
Psamtek II	595–589	Xerxes I	486–465	Nepherites I	399–393		
Apries	589–570	Artaxerxes I	465–424	Hakor	393–380		
Ahmose II	570–526	Darius II	424–405	Nepherites II	c. 380		
Psamtek III	526–525	Artaxerxes II	405–359				

Old Kingdom

c. 2686–2613 BCE	c. 2613–2494 BCE	c. 2494–2345 BCE	c. 2345–2181 BCE
3rd Dynasty	**4th Dynasty**	**5th Dynasty**	**6th Dynasty**
Sanakht 2686–2667	Sneferu 2613–2589	Userkaf 2494–2487	Teti 2345–2323
Djoser 2667–2648	Khufu 2589–2566	Sahura 2487–2475	Userkara 2323–2321
Sekhemkhet 2648–2640	Radjedef 2566–2558	Neferirkara 2475–2455	Pepy I 2321–2287
Khaba 2640–2637	Khafra 2558–2532	Shepseskara 2455–2448	Merenre 2287–2278
Huni 2637–2613	Menkaura 2532–2503	Raneferef 2448–2445	Pepy II 2278–2184
	Shepseskaf 2503–2494	Nyuserra 2445–2421	Nitocris* 2184–2181
		Menkauhor 2421–2414	
		Djedkara 2414–2375	
		Unas 2375–2345	

Giza pyramids

Second Intermediate Period

c. 1985–1795 BCE	c. 1795–1650 BCE	c. 1650–1550 BCE	c. 1650–1550 BCE
12th Dynasty	**13th Dynasty**	**15th Dynasty**	**17th Dynasty**
Amenemhat I 1985–1955	1795–c. 1725	Salitis	In addition to the pharaohs of the 15th and 16th dynasties, several kings ruled from Thebes, including the following:
Senusret I ‡ 1965–1920		Khyan 1600	
Amenemhat II 1922–1878	**14th Dynasty**	Apepi 1555	
Senusret II ‡ 1880–1874	1750–1650	Khamudi	
Senusret III ‡ 1874–1855			Intef
Amenemhat III 1855–1808		**16th Dynasty**	Ta I
Amenemhat IV 1808–1799	Minor figures who ruled at the same time as the 13th dynasty	1650–1550	Seqenenre Taa II c. 1560
Sobekneferu* 1799–1795			Kamose 1555–1550
		Minor Hyksos kings who ruled at the same time as the 15th Dynasty	
Overlaps in dates indicate periods of co-regency			

Third Intermediate Period / Late Period

c. 1069–945 BCE	c. 945–715 BCE	c. 818–715 BCE	c. 747–656 BCE
21st Dynasty	**22nd Dynasty**	**23rd Dynasty**	**25th Dynasty**
Smendes 1069–1043	Sheshonq I 945–924	Several continuous lines of rulers based at Herakleopolis Magna, Hermopolis Magna, Leontopolis, and Tanis, including the following:	Piy 747–716
Amenemnisu 1043–1039	Osorkon I 924–889		Shabaqo 716–702
Psusennes I 1039–991	Sheshonq II c. 890		Shabitqo 702–690
Amenemope 993–984	Takelot I 889–874		Taharqo 690–664
Osorkon the Elder 984–978	Osorkon II 874–850		Tanutamani 664–656
Siamun 978–959	Takelot II 850–825	Pedubastist I 818–793	
Psusennes II 959–945	Sheshonq III 825–773	Sheshonq IV c. 780	
	Pimay 773–767	Osorkon III 777–749	
	Sheshonq V 767–730		
	Osorkon IV 730–715	**24th Dynasty**	
		Bakenrenef 727–715	

Ivory sphinx

Ptolemaic Period

c. 343–332 BCE	c. 332–305 BCE	c. 305–80 BCE	c. 80–30 BCE
Persian Period 2	**Macedonian Dynasty**	**Ptolemaic Dynasty**	**Ptolemaic Dynasty (cont.)**
Artaxerxes III Ochus 343–338	Alexander the Great 332–323	Ptolemy I 305–285	
Arses 338–336	Philip Arrhidaeus 323–317	Ptolemy II 285–246	Ptolemy XI 80
Darius III Codoman 336–332	Alexander IV 317–305	Ptolemy III 246–221	Ptolemy XII 80–51
		Ptolemy IV 221–205	Cleopatra VII* 51–30
		Ptolemy V 205–180	Ptolemy XIII 51–47
		Ptolemy VI 180–145	Ptolemy XIV 47–44
		Ptolemy VII 145	Ptolemy XV 44–30
		Ptolemy VIII 170–116	
		Ptolemy IX 116–107	
		Ptolemy X 107–88	
		Ptolemy XI 88–80	

Lotus flower motif

Egypt became part of the Roman Empire in 30 BCE

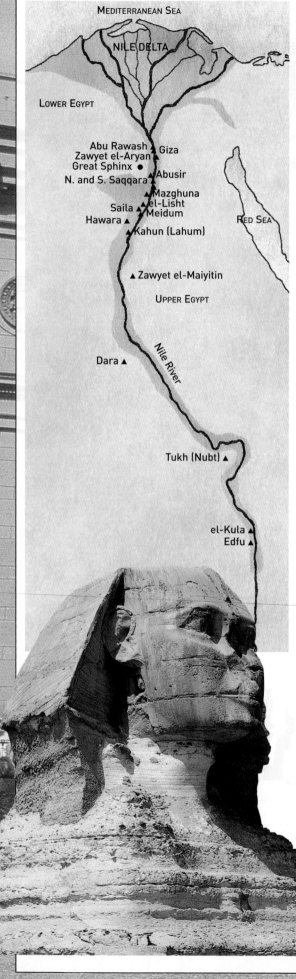

Find out more

If you are inspired to explore the mysteries of ancient Egypt even further, you could go your local museum to see if it has a specialized collection. You can also look at the many websites relating to ancient Egypt. One of the world's finest collections is housed in the Egyptian Museum in Cairo. Founded in 1863, this institution owns over 250,000 objects, many of which are artifacts unearthed in the tomb of King Tutankhamun.

Vulture and cobra symbols

Egyptian Museum
The Egyptian Museum in Cairo does not look especially large, but its thousands of exhibits are very densely packed. The present building, opened in 1902, was designed specifically for this collection.

The Sphinx
Built around 2500 BCE, the Sphinx is the earliest-known monumental sculpture in Egypt. The statue's false beard and nose were lost many centuries ago.

Fine jewelry

Made out of gold and semiprecious stones, ancient Egyptian jewelry is beautifully designed and crafted. Stunning pieces can be seen in many museums around the world.

Gold rings

Section of a girdle

Anubis, jackal-god of embalming

Fish-shaped amulet

Gold star from diadem (headband)

Egypt, American style

The Luxor hotel in Las Vegas has an artificial Nile River, virtual-reality settings, and plastic palm trees (above). Built in a pyramid shape 30 stories tall, it is guarded by a replica of the Giza Sphinx.

King's coffin

Tutankhamun's mummy was placed in three gold nesting coffins. The middle coffin, now in the Egyptian Museum, is made of gilded wood inlaid with turquoise and crimson glass and blue pottery.

Crook and flail

Household objects

Made from colored ceramic in c. 1450 BCE, this wide jar adorned with ducks is typical of the Ancient Egyptian artifacts on view in many museums.

PLACES TO VISIT

EGYPTIAN MUSEUM, CAIRO, EGYPT

The museum has an impressive display of antiquities including:
- the Tutankhamun collection, which contains around 1,700 items relating to the boy king, such as his funeral mask.
- the Royal Mummy Room, where the remains of great rulers can be seen. (Also worth visiting are the Luxor Museum and the Mummification Museum, both in Luxor, Upper Egypt.)

METROPOLITAN MUSEUM OF ART, NEW YORK, NEW YORK

The large Egyptian collection includes:
- sculptures of Queen Hatshepsut, who seized power in the 16th century BCE.
- more than 20 tiny, perfect models from the tomb of a courtier named Mekutra.
- an impressive collection of jewelry.

MUSEUM OF FINE ARTS, BOSTON

The over 40,000 items include:
- a superb collection of artifacts, collected from their original setting.
- a lifelike statue of King Menkaura and his favorite wife, Khamerernebty.

ROYAL ONTARIO MUSEUM, TORONTO, CANADA

The Egyptian gallery in this museum traces Egyptian history from 4000 BCE to 324 BCE. It features:
- computer animation that takes you inside the Great Pyramid.
- the mummy of a temple musician who died in c. 850 BCE.

BRITISH MUSEUM, LONDON, UK

The museum houses the largest collection of ancient Egyptian art outside Cairo, including:
- the Rosetta Stone, used to decipher ancient Egyptian hieroglyphics.
- a gallery of monumental sculpture containing a statue of Ramesses II.
- a display of mummies and coffins.

USEFUL WEBSITES

- Specialized site run by the British Museum:
  www.ancientegypt.co.uk
- General information site, which includes a children's page:
  www.neferchichi.com
- Discovery Channel site, featuring games and virtual tours:
  www.dsc.discovery.com/guides/history/egypt/html
- Award-winning site from the Museum of Fine Art, Boston:
  www.mfa.org/egypt/collections/ancient-world
- Ancient Egypt section of the Royal Ontario Museum site:
  www.rom.on.ca/en/education/online-activities/ancient-egypt

Glossary

ADZE Tool for carving and planing wood.

AMULET Charm used to ward off evil.

ANCIENT EGYPT The period when Egypt was ruled by pharaohs, between c. 3100 BCE to 30 BCE.

ANKH Ancient Egyptian symbol of life that traditionally only gods and royalty carried.

ANTECHAMBER Small room that leads to a more important one.

ARCHEOLOGY The study of history through the excavation and analysis of objects and artifacts.

BA The essence of a deceased person's personality, often represented by his or her head on the body of a hawk. (*see also* KA)

BRECCIA Mottled rock formed of stones cemented together in lime.

CANOPIC JAR Container for storing the internal organs of a dead body.

Ankh

Canopic jars

CARTOUCHE In Egyptology, an oval border around a pharaoh's name.

CASSIA Bark from a type of laurel tree, dried and used in perfume and incense.

CATARACT Powerful rush of water around a large rock that blocks a river's flow. There are several along the Nile.

CROOK Royal symbol in the form of a hooked shepherd's staff representing kingship. (*see also* FLAIL)

DELTA The roughly triangular-shaped area of deposited soil at the mouth of a river.

DEMOTIC SCRIPT A rapid form of writing based on hieratic script. (*see also* HIERATIC SCRIPT and HIEROGLYPHS)

DYNASTY Succession of rulers from related families.

EMBALMING The preservation of a dead body from decay using chemicals, perfumes, salts, and ointments.

FINIAL Decorative emblem or knob on the end of a pole.

FLAIL Royal symbol in the form of a corn-threshing tool that represents the fertility of the land. (*see also* CROOK)

FLAX Flowering plant cultivated for its textile fibers, which are spun into linen cloth.

Crook

Flail

Statue from Karnak with crook and flail

FRANKINCENSE Fragrant gum resin burned as incense. It comes from trees of the genus *Boswellia*.

Henna

GIRDLE Belt or cord worn low on the waist and often adorned with precious stones, shells, silver, and gold.

HENNA Dried and ground-up leaves of a tropical shrub used to color hair and skin and believed by the ancient Egyptians to protect against danger.

HIERATIC SCRIPT A simplified version of hieroglyphs. (*see also* HIEROGLYPHS and DEMOTIC SCRIPT)

HIEROGLYPHS Picture-writing used to build up words in ancient Egyptian script. (*see also* HIERATIC SCRIPT and DEMOTIC SCRIPT)

INCENSE Gum or spice that is burned to create sweet-smelling smoke. The Egyptians used incense in their religious rituals and to purify the air in the temple.

KA A dead person's spirit, which the ancient Egyptians believed could bring his or her body back to life. (*see also* BA)

Lotus flower

KOHL Black powder used to create dramatic eye makeup.

LAPIS LAZULI Bright blue semiprecious stone widely used in Egyptian jewelry and artifacts.

LOTUS Water lily whose shape was widely used in Egyptian art.

MUMMY Dead body that has been preserved from decay, either naturally or by artificial means.

NATRON Moisture-absorbing salt used to dry a corpse before it was wrapped in bandages.

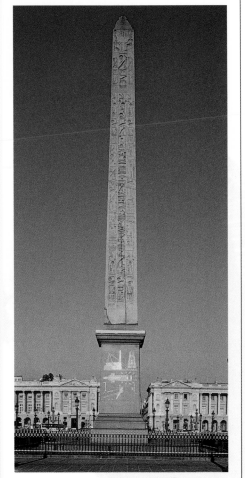

Egyptian obelisk in Paris

NEMES Special striped headcloth worn by Egyptian kings.

OBELISK Tapered stone column with a square or rectangular base and sloping sides rising to a pointed tip.

PALETTE Flat surface on which colors were mixed to make either writing pigments or cosmetics.

PAPYRUS Tall riverside reed whose stem was widely used to make baskets, sandals, boats, rope, and paperlike sheets or scrolls. Papyrus was the main material for writing on in ancient Egypt.

PECTORAL Ornamental pendant or similar piece of jewelry, often decorated with a metal framework inset with glass or semiprecious stones.

PHARAOH The title given to the rulers of ancient Egypt. The word pharaoh means "great house," and originally referred to the king's palace.

PYRAMID Massive stone structure with a square base and sloping sides. Pyramids were usually royal tombs, but some may have had other purposes.

REGENT Court official or minor royal—often the king's mother appointed to rule on behalf of a very young pharaoh.

SARCOPHAGUS Elaborate and massive outer stone coffin.

SCARAB Sacred dung beetle that symbolized the Sun-god Khepri.

SCRIBE Government official who, unlike most ordinary people, could both read and write.

SENET Egyptian board game based on the struggle between good and evil.

SHABTI Figures made in the image of servants and buried with important people so they could perform any manual tasks required in the afterlife.

SHADUF Pole with bucket and counterweight used for raising water from the Nile to fill irrigation canals.

SHRINE Container for holding the statue of a god or the remains of a dead body; a place dedicated to the memory of a dead person.

SICKLE Crescent-shaped tool used for harvesting grain.

SIDELOCK Section of hair anchored on one side of the head to indicate the youth of the wearer.

SISTRUM Ceremonial rattle carried by noblewomen and priestesses.

SITULA Sacred vessel that contained holy water for the temple.

SNAKE Egyptian game involving counters and a circular stone board representing a snake coiled around its own head.

SOUL HOUSE Miniature model dwelling placed in the tomb of its dead owner for use in the afterlife.

SPHINX In ancient Egypt, the sphinx was a monumental creature with a lion's body and the head of the ruler. Sphinxes were believed to guard the entrances to the underworld on both the eastern and the western horizons.

Shabti figures

STELA Upright stone slab or pillar covered with carvings or inscriptions.

THROWSTICK Wooden hunting instrument similar to a boomerang, used to stun, injure, or kill prey.

TOMB Grave, monument, or building where the body of a dead person is laid.

UNDERWORLD Abode of the dead, thought to lie deep under the earth.

URAEUS The royal cobra, displayed by pharaohs on the front of the head. The serpent was believed to spit fire at the king's enemies.

WADJET EYE Protective symbol representing the eye of Horus.

WINNOWING The process of separating the chaff from the grain by tossing both in the air.

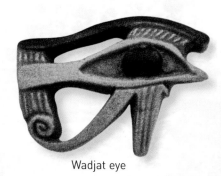

Wadjat eye

Index

Acknowledgments

Dorling Kindersley would like to thank:
The Department of Egyptian Antiquities, British Museum for the provision of artifacts for photography; James Putnam for his invaluable assistance in arranging for artifacts to be photographed and for his help with picture research; Celia Clear of British Museum Publications; the Departments of Oriental Antiquities and Medieval and Later Antiquities, British Museum for extra objects for photography; Morgan Reid for his advice on photographic lighting; Meryl Silbert for production; Karl Shone for special photography (pp. 20–21); Lester Cheeseman for his desktop publishing expertise; Kathy Lockley for picture research.

Illustrators: Thomas Keenes: 21tl, 32br, 33bl, 43t, 55bc; Eugene Fleury: 8cl

For this edition, the publisher would also like to thank: Hazel Beynon for text editing, and Carron Brown for proofreading.

The publisher would like to thank the following for their kind permission to reproduce their images:
a=above, b=bottom, c=center, far=far, l=left, m=middle, r= right, t=top

Agyptisches Museum/Photo: Staatliche Museen zu Berlin: 48bl. Ancient Art & Architecture Collection: 10bl, 10 bm, 11tr, 11 bl, 14tr, 28–9t. Anglo Aquarium Plant Co./Barbara Thomas: 26ml. Bridgeman Art Library: 24tr, 28tl, 28br. British Museum: 6b, 9tr, 10m, 11m, 14br, 15tl, 15tm, 15br, 16tr, 18m, 19t, 19br, 22tl, 26mr, 27tl, 27mr, 28m, 29r, 30mr, 32, 33, 34m, 35mr, 40tl, 41t, 41bm, 44m, 45tl, 46l,46b, 49bl, 50m, 51tm, 53tm, 56tl, 56bl, 57br, 58bm, 59bm, 60tr, 60lm, 62bl, 62bm, 63tr. British Museum/Nina M. de Garis Davies: 39m, 48mr, 51b, 61m. Peter Clayton: 26tl, 38m. Bruce Coleman Ltd: 41mr. Michael Dixon, Photo Resources: 10tr, 25tl. Egypt Exploration Society, London: 54br. Mary Evans Picture Library: 57tr, 62tr. Werner Forman Archive: 8tr. Editions Gallimard: 20tl. Griffith Institute, Ashmolean Museum, Oxford: 23b. Robert Harding Picture Library: 12ml, 13bl, 23mr, 24bl, 36–7b, 39tr, 42tl, 53ml, 54tl. George Hart: 23m, 29m. Michael Holford: 41br. Hutchison Library: 9mr. Courtesy of the Oriental Institute of the University of Chicago: 44-5b. Popperfoto: 38tl. James Putnam: 31ml. Louvre/© Kéunion des Musées Nationaux: 55tm. Uni-Dia Verlag: 43 ml. University College, London: 22b, 35ml. Roger Wood: 32tl. Verlag Philipp von Zabern/ Cairo Museum: 8–9b.

All other images © Dorling Kindersley. For further information see: www.dkimages.com